YOU CAN

Make the MOST of READING

Kate Ruttle

FOR AGES

4-11

❝We believe that reading can transform people's lives.❞
The Reading Agency

372.
412
Rut

Acknowledgements

Author
Kate Ruttle

Editor
Nicola Morgan

Development Editor
Kate Pedlar

Project Editor
Fabia Lewis

Series Designer
Catherine Perera

Cover Designer
Allison Parry, Anna Oliwa

Cover photography
© iofoto/www.stockxpert.com

Design
Q2A Media

Text © Kate Ruttle
© 2009, Scholastic Ltd

Designed using Adobe InDesign

Published by Scholastic Ltd
Villiers House
Clarendon Avenue
Leamington Spa
Warwickshire CV32 5PR

www.scholastic.co.uk

Printed by Bell and Bain Ltd.
1 2 3 4 5 6 7 8 9 9 0 1 2 3 4 5 6 7 8

British Library Cataloguing-in-Publication Data
A catalogue record for this book is available from the British Library.
ISBN 978-1407-11446-0

Mixed Sources
Product group from well-managed forests and other controlled sources
www.fsc.org Cert no. TT-COC-002769
© 1996 Forest Stewardship Council
FSC

Contents

Contents

Introduction

Children in the 21st century have unparalleled opportunities for occupying their leisure time and there is significant evidence that fewer and fewer are becoming readers. There is also evidence that young adults who haven't become readers at school are unlikely to adopt the habit of reading. We owe it to our children not just to give them opportunities to read, but to make the most of reading in primary school in order to give children opportunities and encouragement to become readers.

Multimedia

As teachers today we have unparalleled opportunities for teaching reading: we have access to all of the same technologies that the children have access to and we can use the technologies to excite the children and as prompts for reading. The reading curriculum we can offer children is now vast and includes a range of media. In addition to reading books, we can now teach children about reading for games and ICT, to enhance their enjoyment of film, to understand and enjoy poetry, to access music, to explore their culture and heritage through reading – as well as reading for pleasure.

Cross curricular

As the literacy curriculum evolves, so does recognition that cross-curricular approaches to learning help children to make connections between what they already know and what they are learning: reading is generally at the heart of cross-curricular work. For this reason, this book is organised into themes. Whatever the passions of you and your children there will be at least one theme which can cater for you. The ideas in this book can be used to provide starting points for your own reading adventures with your class. You know your children as no-one else does. Take your class with you on reading-inspired journeys into worlds that we don't explore often enough with our over-crowded curriculum

All of the themes are relevant to the Early Years Foundation Stage (EYFS) and Primary curricula, but they encourage us to extend our reading behaviours beyond books to include ICT, film, art, sport, the media and our culture and heritage. A chart showing how the activities in this book are relevant to the rest of the curriculum is included on page 63.

Within this book

This book contains 53 units of work. The units are paired, so that there is always one for KS1 and a matched idea for KS2. Some of the ideas will be familiar, but many will be new. The activities as described may not be exactly right for your class, but that doesn't matter. The intention is to provide some stimulus ideas – together with websites for free and appropriate resources – that you can use to plan exciting forays into the world of reading with your class. These ideas are intended as starting points to provide teachers with the excuse we need to nurture our own creativity and to harness it to the children's interests and enthusiasm in order that we can give our children the best start to life as well as the most important and exciting gift.

No matter what the age and reading attainment of your children, grab any opportunity to engage, excite and enthuse them as they explore reading through fiction, non-fiction and reference books, as well as ICT resources, film, storytelling, drama and personal stories. With the help of this book, I hope that You Can Make the Most of Reading.

P.S. Teachers in Scotland, Wales and Northern Ireland

Hello. You haven't been forgotten. Although some specific links to the English curriculum are mentioned, they are all spelled out in words rather than reference numbers so they will be easy to link to your curriculum. It is important, therefore, to note that all of the ideas are appropriate for all children, wherever they may live in the UK.

You Can... Provide daily opportunities to read in F/KS1

How do you create daily opportunities for your children to enjoy sustained exposure to reading? Even those who can't yet read will benefit from opportunities to engage with books. The challenge we have is to engage all of the children, not just those who enjoy books because their parents have books at home.

Thinking points
● What can you do to ensure that all children in your class are hooked into reading?

● Are there children in your class who are not passionate about reading? Do you know why? Try talking to them about their reading habits, who reads to them, when and where they read. Who else do they see reading during the day at home?

● Use information from your interviews to address the root causes for lack of interest. Do you need to consider lending books to the families? Would games based around the books help? Would the children benefit from access to puppets to role play the stories?

● Focus on what you can change or influence, not on what you can't.

Recommended websites
● http://storynory.com/ provides free audio books for children to listen to (although you do have to listen to adverts first).

● http://kids.audible.com provides a wide range of downloadable texts in MP3 format (many of which are American).

● http://lightupyourbrain.com has a wide selection of free, downloadable stories, many of which are familiar, and includes modern classics.

● http://www.candlelightstories.com/ has a wider selection of stories, including many from a variety of cultures.

Tips, ideas and activities
● Is your book corner as attractive as it can be? If possible, put cushions and beanbags in your book corner so that children can sit comfortably with books. Make sure that the books are well displayed and that tatty or torn books are taken out of the book corner as promptly as possible.

● Provide a tent or make a tent-like area using a drape from the ceiling to create a quiet place for children to escape to with their books. Present this opportunity as a treat, so that children begin to value the opportunity to go and have some quiet time with their book.

● Use technologies to allow children access to audio books. These enable children to listen to stories individually or in groups while they read the book or look at the pictures. New technologies allow children to listen to books on MP3 headphones as well as conventional CD players.

● Read aloud to your children. How often do you read aloud to your class just for the pleasure of sharing a high quality book? There tend to be ulterior motives for books read in literacy lessons and many children become wary of them for this reason. End-of-the-day stories are often hurried and curtailed by home time, letters to give out, lost coats. A story at the beginning of the afternoon, however, can be read just for its own sake. Time can be made for children to discuss it, to talk about their reactions, to explore the language and the pictures. Although the curriculum is very crowded, do you have time not to prioritise reading?

● Read non-fiction as well as fiction. Many young children – particularly boys – find stories too demanding on their memories, so they switch off. By reading high quality non-fiction, where the chunks of information are short and the illustrations are clear on the page, these children can be persuaded that books are for them too.

You Can... Provide sustained opportunities to read in KS2

Thinking points

● Many schools have some kind of silent/guided/group reading opportunities at the beginning of the afternoon. These are often about 15 minutes long and that time includes giving books out, finding lost belongings and sorting out problems from dinner-time play.

● Talk to your children about their views on this time. Is it long enough? Is it too long? Would they rather have fewer, longer opportunities to read? Are they happy with the opportunities you give them?

● Try to create opportunities following the guidance of your class. Young readers often know what they need to nurture their interest in reading.

Curriculum and Framework links

Books you choose to share with the class can be cross curricular and focused around literacy genres, but don't forget to choose books that are just great books!

Extracts are no longer encouraged by the Primary Strategy and teachers are encouraged to take time to read with children and to let children read.

Year 3 – Share and compare reasons for reading preferences, extending the range of books read.

Year 4 – Read extensively favourite authors or genres and experiment with other types of text.

Year 5 – Reflect on reading habits and preferences and plan personal reading goals.

Year 6 – Read extensively and discuss personal reading with others, including in reading groups.

Year 6 – Sustain engagement with longer texts, using different techniques to make the text come alive.

Michael Rosen, former Children's Laureate, condemned the teaching of reading in KS2 as 'excerptitis'. He complained that many children are put off reading because their exposure to books is limited to reading extracts and bite-sized samples of writing. Children who come from literate homes are more likely to have additional opportunities to become readers out of school, but what about the rest? How can they be persuaded to become readers?

Tips, ideas and activities

● Find out from your class about their attitudes to reading opportunities in school. What do they like or dislike? Is there something they think you could be doing or provide to make reading a higher priority and to give it a greater status in your class?

● Read to your children as often as possible – and not just at the end of Friday afternoon. Read longer novels that you enjoy and that are on the cusp of most children's independent reading. Select novels for particular classes, recognising that they have different likes and dislikes. Create opportunities to discuss the books that you are reading together.

● Play together with language from the books that you read together. Let words that have taken your fancy roll around your tongue. Model enjoying words and phrases, picking them out of the text and repeating them, writing them down, illustrating them, weaving stories and ideas around them, explaining how they make you feel or the images that you see. Readers enjoy words as well as enjoying the stories and pictures.

● Give yourself a half-termly treat by spending a day in a good children's bookshop with a colleague, a friend or family. Talk to the children's book buyer and find out their recommendations for new authors, then sit and read. Does the book grab you? Can you imagine reading it to your class? If not, try a different book!

● Ensure that you read a wide variety of genres, but don't forget poetry and non-fiction. These forms often provide a 'way in' for children who don't always enjoy stories.

● Help children to understand the transformational power of reading. Share your own – or invite a friend or colleague to share if you haven't got the passion yourself – insights into reading and talk about how reading impacts on your life. Let children understand how access into fictional worlds – whether fantasy or not – is exciting and creates new understanding about events in your real world.

You Can... **Use environmental print**

Environmental print is most children's earliest exposure to reading: they generally learn to recognise logos from a very early age and later 'read' signs and labels. Engaging with environmental print establishes a child at the centre of a community of 'readers'.

Thinking points

● A project on environmental print can be a great starting point for links with the community. Invite people who use different kinds of print (in different languages or Braille) into school to share their experiences.

● Teach children to recognise print that is important to them. In Foundation it's likely to include their own name and family roles such as 'Mum' and 'Dad'. By Year 2, it should include their family name, telephone number and address.

● Develop a project about print in art or ICT. Link these projects across the curriculum and allow children to create print responses.

Links to Letters and Sounds

Environmental print is an excellent place to practise many principles.

● Phase 1: look for alliteration in adverts and rhymes in jingles.

● Phase 2: look at simple signage such as: 'cat' or 'dog' on pet bowls; 'fish and chips' on food packaging.

● Phase 3/4: look at food packaging to find examples of most of the graphemes you need children to recognise and begin to introduce longer words. Look at signage in and around the school.

● Phase 5/6: focus on names as well as more complex signage in school and in the community.

Tips, ideas and activities

● Ask children to bring print material from their homes into school. This can include books, but should also include other print, for example: phone directories, recipes, comics, television listings, newspapers, junk mail and packaging.

● Let children use data-handling tools on a computer to sort the print according to different criteria. Let older children choose their own criteria but give younger ones hints such as: *How many colours are used? How many different kinds of font are used? How many languages are used?*

● Discuss the different purposes of print. Can the children work out who might want to read the different kinds of printed material and why?

● Go on an 'environmental print' walk around school. If children have access to digital cameras, allow them to take the camera(s) with them and snap as many different kinds of print as they can. Discuss the purpose of, and audience for, each of the different kinds of print.

● If possible, take the children and a camera into your community and talk about the environmental print they see. Use 'print' in its widest meaning to include signs and logos. Each time you see print, record it with a photograph or drawing and bring it back into school.

● Sort the print collected on environmental print walks according to purpose and audience. Raise children's awareness that every piece of print has a clear purpose and audience and that this will determine what it looks like and what it contains.

● Making children aged 4–7 aware of print in its myriad of forms will be a great starting point for their own reading and writing journeys.

You Can... **Use newspapers**

Newspapers are found in many houses; from free papers to broadsheets. Sometimes religious and other community groups have their own newspapers and in many areas newspapers are written in different languages. Local papers are often central to the community: they not only advertise events but also highlight local stories and community campaigns. Begin the National Year of Reading by putting the community at the heart of reading.

Thinking points

● Look at community issues in a newspaper and invite someone who is involved with the issue (such as a new housing development) to explain how the newspaper has helped or hindered their cause.

● Visit offices of a local newspaper.

● Teaching children how to use and to read newspapers can provide reluctant readers with a 'way in' to reading. Texts can be quite short and are often illustrated with pictures. The brevity of newspaper headlines can engage some reluctant readers.

Framework links

Although newspapers are not a recommended text type in every year, they can often be used to reinforce specific objectives.

● Strands 1–4: Use newspapers for speaking and listening activities, such as information for debates.

● Strands 5–6: Use headlines as the basis for reading and phonics work; use articles and highlighter pens for spelling investigations.

● Strands 7–8: Use newspaper stories as free model texts to explore shaping a text in a given number of words, using bias, creating interest or informing.

● Strands 9–10: Let the children write stories and create their own newspaper, linking to ICT.

Tips, ideas and activities

● Ask children to bring (old!) newspapers into school. Suggest that they bring as many different types of newspaper as they can collect in their house. This should ensure that you gather the variety of newspapers that are available in your community.

● Introduce technical language children will need to talk about newspapers. www.nnieag.org.uk/glossary.htm provides a useful glossary of relevant terms from which you can select those that are most relevant for the age of your class.

● Together, look through the newspapers and discuss features they all have in common. Can children distinguish adverts from stories? Do they know the function of the different sizes and fonts? Can they work out how to follow a story through the paper?

● Make a database of newspaper features. Discuss why some features are common to most or all newspapers whereas some are less common. What distinguishes them?

● Look at the organisation of the newspapers. Traditionally, sport has been at the back of the paper. *Is that true for your selection? Where are regular features like television listings and weather?* Is there a rationale that the children can detect for where in the newspaper different stories are placed?

● Let groups of children choose a story from their newspaper and then follow it up first in other newspapers and then online. *Is the same information consistently available?* Discuss what might prompt different publications to make different decisions regarding what to write about. In particular, focus on sports reports. *Why might a local paper in one part of the country present a football match report differently to another paper?*

● Look at headlines and discuss how the words in them are chosen. *Are any of the headlines particularly eye-catching or memorable?* Discuss what makes them so.

You Can... **Sell it!**

Children are brought up in a world where advertisements surround them; but do they realise what they are for? Teaching children to recognise the purpose of advertisements helps them understand how they are being drawn in to wanting something. Simply teaching very young children to ask questions about an advert will begin to lay a foundation for being critical readers of adverts.

Thinking points

● Teaching children to ask questions can be tricky. Use the hierarchy of question difficulty, which begins with *what*, *which* and *who*, and progresses through *why* to the hardest question, *how*. Model asking questions.

● Be aware that if you teach children to question what they hear and see, you may experience some more awkward questions that you'd rather children didn't ask. You may want to establish class expectations about questioning.

● Develop questioning through stories. This can lead to independent research projects and philosophical discussions.

EYFS and Framework links

● EYFS, KUW/CLL: focus on asking questions and finding out more about their literary world. Children see adverts around them all the time, without realising their purpose. Encourage oral language development as they enjoy talking about their toys.

● Years 1 and 2: link to work on information texts and explanations. What kind of information do adverts give us? How is an advert the same as, and different from, a non-chronological report text about a toy? Try writing both and comparing them. Focus on the type of information given *and* the language used.

Tips, ideas and activities

● Can any of the children find an advert for a toy which they own? Ask them to talk about the toy: *what are its good points? What are the problems with it?* Compare the child's experience of the toy to the advert.

● Talk about the kind of information given in the advert. *Is there a picture of the toy? Why is a picture useful?* Discuss why this information was selected. *Is this information likely to make you want to buy the toy or not?* Look at the language used. *Are there any exciting, descriptive words?*

● Can children think of any more information about the toy they would like to ask? For example:
   ● Ask about the size: *is it as big as it looks in the advert?*
   ● Ask about its use: *how difficult is it to operate the toy and make it do all the things that it appears to do in the advert?*
   ● Ask about its durability: *how easy is it to break the toy?*
   ● Ask about its fun value: *for how long would you want to play with it?*

● Choose a toy from the classroom that isn't played with very much. Can the children think of things they could say about the toy in an advert? Why would they include this information? What kind of information would they *not* choose to include? Why not?

● Ask children to create their own advertisement for a toy. They could either draw a picture of the toy or base their work around a digital photograph or image from the internet. What kind of information are they going to give about the toy? Encourage the use of at least one descriptive word to make the toy sound very desirable.

You Can... **Judge the advert**

Children are constantly exposed to advertising on television, in the built environment and in print. Help them to recognise an advert when they see it and to understand that someone is trying to sell them something. Ask children to bring in catalogues and print adverts for toys in order to explore them in class. Focus on adverts that give information rather than just a price.

Thinking points

● Can children list key features of adverts? How long do they think an advert is? Discuss whether or not cartoon series like *Power Rangers* are anything more than extended adverts.

● The power of advertising lies in convincing your audience that you know what is right for them; the only antidote is healthy scepticism. Teach your children to question what they read, see and hear so that they can draw their own conclusions.

● There are strict guidelines as to what can be shown on children's television. Older children might like to debate the value of this.

Speaking and listening links

● Year 3: present their own information gleaned from newspapers; ask and answer questions; follow up points in group and whole class discussion.

● Year 4: present their views then offer reasons and evidence; evaluate the contributions of music, words and images to adverts.

● Year 5: work in groups to present their own radio advert, sequencing points logically; evaluate each other's use of persuasive language.

● Year 6: use techniques of dialogic talk to evaluate adverts; analyse and evaluate how speakers present points effectively.

Tips, ideas and activities

● Ask children to collect printed advertisements for toys, computer games, books and comics. The advertisements can come from newspapers, magazines, comics, catalogues, junk mail or be printed from the internet.

● As a class, discuss some of the features of the advertisements they have been collecting. Give some prompts if the children need them, but try to encourage them to develop their own ideas. Features might include, for example:
  ● Use of pictures and use of children in the pictures.
  ● Use of colour in both print and pictures.
  ● Different fonts and font sizes.
  ● Flashes saying 'New' or 'Sale'.
  ● Logos and slogans.
  ● Bullet points.
  ● Exciting adjectives or adverbs.

● Talk about the audience of the adverts. *Which ones are written for children and which for their parents? How can you tell?*

● Discuss the purpose of the adverts; *they are all trying to sell to you but how are they doing it? Is it because the product is 'educational' or 'healthy'? Is it to do with the amount of fun you can have? Is this product better/ cheaper/ longer lasting than a competitor?* Try to identify how the advert is trying to work.

● Work together to draw up a checklist of things to look out for in a 'successful' advert. First, define what a 'successful' advert might be. Then make a list of key features.

● Let groups of children use the list to compare, contrast and rank up to five advertisements. In addition to ticking off items on the checklist, they should also write a brief commentary on the advert so that others can understand the rationale for their judgements.

● The whole class can then listen to feedback and ask questions.

● Take a vote on each group's highest ranking advert. Present a class award to the advert that is considered the most successful.

You Can... Put nursery rhymes in the news

Encourage parents and carers to look through local newspapers with their children, particularly if they share an interest, such as a sport or local news story. Let children bring in some of the news stories that interest them, particularly in the local news.

Thinking points

● Check that your children know common nursery rhymes to use as the basis for their own stories. You may wish to encourage EAL children to do this work in their first language.

● This kind of project is a good one to work on as a home–school project with parents who feel less confident about reading. The context of Humpty Dumpty is fairly unthreatening. To emphasise that some newspapers have cartoon strips, children and parents could create a Humpty Dumpty cartoon strip as a joint project.

● More independent learners can be encouraged to create their own publications around different nursery rhymes or other texts.

Links to Letters and Sounds

● Phase 1/2: focus on rhyme – make sets of rhyming words; explore the implications of changing 'wall' to 'box' or to 'chair'. How might the rhyme change?

● Phase 3/4: focus on syllables and rhythm – *how many syllables in Humpty Dumpty? How many two-syllable words in the whole rhyme?* Clap the rhythm of *'all the king's horses and all the king's men'*.

● Phase 5/6: Look at, for example: the word ending on *Humpty;* the sound of the three adjacent consonants *mpt;* different ways of representing the phoneme */or/;* short vowel phonemes.

Tips, ideas and activities

● Agree a nursery rhyme as the basis for a shared reading and writing session. 'Humpty Dumpty' is probably the easiest. Write the words for all the children to read.

● 'Unpick' the written code to enable children to read the rhyme (see links to *Letters and Sounds*, below).

● Revisit the rhyme to look at the meaning and encourage children to ask questions about the events in the rhyme. As far as possible, let the children ask the questions. Younger ones may need a little prompting, for example:
  ○ *Why was Humpty Dumpty on the wall?*
  ○ *Are there many egg-people around in the world?*
  ○ *What was he doing that made him fall off the wall?*

● Ask children to chat with a talk partner to begin to generate answers to the questions.

● Use role play to further expand on the questions and answers. Let the children work in pairs: they can take turns to be Humpty Dumpty on the wall and one of the King's Men. In role, ask them to explore answers to the questions.

● Let children make photograph storyboards of their role play. They can then use the storyboards as a springboard for writing.

● Show children a glossy magazine format and explain that they are going to be asked to produce an article on Humpty Dumpty for such a publication. Talk about features of the articles such as:
  ○ Photographs and pictures.
  ○ A heading.
  ○ Short paragraphs of text.

● Ask children to use illustrations and their photograph stories to make and publish their own 'Humpty Dumpty' magazine.

● The writing can include mark making or can be carried out using ICT writing supports as necessary.

You Can... **Rewrite nursery rhyme history**

Nursery Rhymes are ideal places to start a career in journalism. The stories are easy and accessible so none of your budding journalists can complain that they can't think of any ideas. If you have children from many cultures in your classroom, ask them to share nursery rhymes and household rhymes from their own cultures. They can share them in their own language or in English.

Thinking points

● Use music lessons to explore rhythms and ensure that children know the lyrics of common nursery rhymes.

● Use nursery rhymes as the basis for clapping games. Children can recite the rhymes while clapping the beat: individually first and then with a partner.

● Explore the implications of rewriting nursery rhymes in other poetry styles such as rap. How would this impact on the rhythm and lyrics?

● Explore the history of nursery rhymes. There are a number of websites such as www.rhymes-org.uk that can be used to provide some background information.

Framework links

● Year 3: adventure and mystery stories – adapt the headline as a chapter heading and write the story as suggested.

● Year 4: explanations – explore the chronology of the events leading up to, or starting from, the fall. (Build on the Newspaper topic in Non-fiction Unit 1)

● Year 5: persuasive writing – write the same story from different perspectives. Introduce the idea of bias in newspaper reports.

● Year 6: journalistic writing.

Tips, ideas and activities

● Agree a nursery rhyme as the basis for a shared writing session. 'Jack and Jill' is probably the easiest.

● Write the words for the children to read. Encourage them to ask questions about the events in the rhyme. As far as possible, let the children ask the questions. Younger ones may need a little prompting, for example:
  ● Why did Jack and Jill have to go *up* a hill to find water?
  ● Is it sensible to build a well on top of a hill?
  ● Where or when did they live?
  ● Why didn't an adult take them up the hill?
  ● Why did Jill fall? Did she trip up? Were Jack and Jill seen to be arguing? Might Jack have pushed Jill?

● Working in groups, children should choose the most interesting question to discuss. Within their groups, ask the children to suggest answers to the questions. They should revisit the text as often as necessary to find any additional clues.

● Use role play to further expand on the activities. Hot seat one child as Jill another as Jack. Another child could be a casual bystander. The other children in the groups should take on the role of investigative reporter. The reporter's role is to find out as much information about the event as possible.

● Let children in the group suggest as many different headlines as possible. Remind them that the job of the headline is to attract a reader's attention and make them want to read on.

● Once the headline is written, ask children to write the newspaper stories. If possible, use computers and teach children how to create and use columns in word processing software.

● Let groups of children select their own nursery rhymes and revisit the same progression of activities.

● Publish the stories in a newspaper titled 'Nursery Rhyme World'.

AGES 4–7

You Can... **Support reading with parents**

Children who read at home with their parents or carers have a better attitude towards reading and are likely to learn to read more quickly. However, many parents don't know how to help their children and in too many homes, the bedtime story has been forgotten: parents are unaware of the important bonding and intellectual engagement of a bedtime story.

Thinking points
● Make resources available to parents in your community who don't read. These can include simple games that are linked to books, tracking activities to ensure eye and hand movement from left to right across the page, wordless books, comics and magazines.

● Reassure all parents that one of the most import aspects of reading at home, especially in these early stages, is the special time for parent-child bonding. If parents don't read, encourage them still to make that special time available each day.

Now try this
● Join Reading Connects (www.literacytrust.org.uk/readingconnects) for free reading leaflets for children and parents.

● Have a special week when you invite dads in to read with the children. Ask a dad to read a poem or story to the whole class. Make sure your boys know that dads read too!

● Make links with your local library. Invite a librarian to come and read to your class. Can you take the children to the library? Can you organise it so that all of your children are members of the local library?

Tips, ideas and activities
● Make a leaflet for parents, explaining to them how to read with their children at different stages. Include advice on how to:
  ○ Sound out words: which part of the word needs to be focused on.
  ○ Correct errors: which kinds of errors to correct, and how.
  ○ Develop reading strategies beyond phonics.
  ○ Talk about books, including both questions about events that happened and more inferential questions beginning, for example: *why…? how do you think…?*
  ○ Make time to read to children when the television isn't competing for attention and reading isn't instead of going outside or playing with friends.

● Have a reading time once a week when, half an hour before the end of the school day, you invite parents into the classroom to read with their child and other children. This can be a very informal occasion, when children can read and respond to books independently or with adults. Opportunities like this may give less confident parents the feeling that they can help and you can model ways of reading with children.

● Make sure that you have a wide variety of attractive classroom library books for children to take home and share with parents.

● Make a selection of bookmarks with advice to parents on reading particular types of books or books at a particular reading level. Send a bookmark every time a book goes home so that the parents can be confident about reading.

● Have a reading evening when you invite parents in to hear how you teach reading in school. Try to invite a guest speaker who can also talk about reading to children.

You Can... Support reading with parents

Many parents believe that their job of hearing children read on a regular basis is 'done' once their children are reasonably competent at reading aloud. Bedtime stories also tend to disappear as children get older. So how can we persuade parents that time spent reading with their 7–11 year old is a good investment of time?

Thinking points

● It's not just parents who stop thinking of reading aloud as important once children leave Key Stage 1. Key Stage 2 is a tricky time for many young readers who are not yet competent to become truly independent readers but who no longer want to be heard reading at home. Keeping them alert, engaged and interested is a challenge in all schools. Why not ask them to help you to meet the challenge? Your children are most likely to have some of the solutions for your school.

● Make good use of your library in order to ensure that it doesn't get 'lost' as someone looks for a place to install a new cloakroom.

Now try this

● Join Reading Connects (www.literacytrust.org.uk/ readingconnects) for free reading leaflets for children and parents.

● Try to have termly reading interviews with each child. Use this opportunity to find out more about both the child's and the parents'/ carers' attitude to reading. Are there parents/carers who are more likely to support reading non-fiction? Or poetry?

● Try to find out where you can buy or borrow a variety of texts that are accessible to all parents in the school. This may include dual language texts, non-English texts or even Braille.

Tips, ideas and activities

● Ask children to keep reading diaries including the widest variety of reading opportunities they have from day to day. Ask for these diaries to be signed and commented on by parents.

● Make a selection of bookmarks with advice to parents on reading particular types of books or books at a particular reading level. Send a bookmark every time a book goes home so that the parents can be confident about how to read the book with their child.

● Set up a reading challenge that includes parents reading a novel to their child. Don't make it a race to finish, but give a reasonable amount of time, for example half a term. At the end of the time, have an awards assembly, with parents invited, and give children certificates. The reading challenge can include:
  ○ A list of fiction genres for children to read. When they have read a book in the genre, they write the title and a brief review.
  ○ A list of non-fiction text types for children to read and use. These can include texts such as recipes, other instructions, television guides, the internet and telephone books as well as recommended text types.
  ○ A novel to be read to the child by parents/ carers.
  ○ A list of other types of media including newspapers, comics and magazines.

● Create a digital presentation including video, digital photographs and book reviews and put it on your website (with parental permission) or show it during open evenings. Let parents know that their child is featured on the presentation to show them how much reading is valued in the school.

● Invite parents to a 'meet the author' event when children, as authors, read from their own writing. Try to be as inclusive as possible and to celebrate a wide variety of types of writing.

You Can... Use reading to answer questions about being healthy

Children aged 4–7 can be encouraged to take some responsibility for their health, but first they need to understand what constitutes a healthy body. Link this topic to science objectives and encourage children to recognise that they use reading for all areas of the curriculum – not just literacy.'

Thinking points
● Deriving information from each different text type involves different skills that may need to be taught.

● When you are choosing charts to share with the children check on the amount of text that will be useful to them. The younger the children, the more likely they are to be confused by extraneous details.

● Take an interest in the children's diet. They are at an ideal age for beginning to introduce ideas about healthy eating but are beginning to know how to use their 'pester-power' at home. Giving them some responsibility for their health and diet may help them to develop more healthy ideas about food.

Links to science
EYFS and QCA:

● EYFS, KUW: Even at this early stage children need to understand that we read for many purposes, including 'finding out'. At this stage children are likely to be able to match words, to recognise print and to understand that when you model reading, you are making meaning from the print.

● Years 1 and 2, Science Units 1A/2A: Ourselves. The suggestions on this page are in line with the activities in the science unit. These activities emphasise and explicitly teach the purpose of reading in order to find out information.

Tips, ideas and activities
● Give children access to a variety of media that will give them information. These can include:
  ○ Charts showing names of body parts, or food groups.
  ○ Photographs with captions.
  ○ Simple books about staying healthy.

● Make use of the internet as well as software for the whiteboard. There are an increasing number of free resources available for schools, for example: www.bbc.co.uk/schools/teachers/ks1/scienceclips.shtml.

● As you refer to different media to find information, or as you give children activities, make the role of reading for finding out explicit. They may be reading logos, book titles, individual words on diagrams or paragraphs of text in books or on screen.

● Teach children how to find the information. Teach the difference between an index and a contents page; show children how to use on-screen menu pages efficiently; emphasise the skills needed to read instructions carefully.

● There are a number of websites containing simple, interactive games about healthy living. Encourage the children to use their reading skills in order to play the games.

● Encourage children to ask questions. At first these are likely to be straightforward but, once young children are used to using their 'questioning muscle', they can begin to explore some quite complex ideas. Talk about how and where they might find answers to their questions.

● Ask children to bring in food labels from packaging at home. Use the labels to construct your own chart of food groups. Talk about strategies for recognising each of the products in the supermarket. *Do you need to read all of the time, or can you use colour and design as an alternative?*

You Can... Use reading to find out about being healthy

Children aged 7–11 should be encouraged to take some responsibility for their health, through healthy eating and understanding the importance of exercise. Reading is the most likely medium to find information about being healthy. Health and sport often mean more to children than reading, so show them how the two are inextricably linked.

Thinking points

● In the light of all the reports on childhood obesity, it becomes increasingly important to teach children about healthy eating. Invite a debate in the class about who is responsible for children's health: them, their parents or schools?

● Use outcomes from your class discussions as the basis for parents' assemblies, class projects, homework topics, and so on. Try to arrange for as much sharing of information and ideas as possible with parents.

● Take the opportunity of looking at healthy eating to explore and compare diets of different community groups in your class.

Links to science

QCA: there is a related science topic in every year group except Year 6.

● Year 3, Unit 3A: Teeth and Eating.

● Year 4, Unit 4A: Moving and Growing.

● Year 5, Unit 5A: Keeping Healthy.

● When linking the ideas on this page to each of the science units, the key idea is to emphasise the importance of reading in finding information. Some children in Key Stage 2 'switch off' to reading because they don't want to read fiction. It is important for these children to understand that developing reading skills is the best way to find information.

Tips, ideas and activities

● Give children access to a variety of media which will give them information. These can include:
  ● Charts showing names of body parts, or food groups.
  ● Labelled diagrams.
  ● Photographs with captions.
  ● Information books about staying healthy.
  ● Interactive 'healthy body' games with instructions.
  ● Online interactive sites.

● As you refer to different media to find information, or as you give children activities, make the role of reading for finding out explicit. The children may be reading logos, book titles, words on diagrams or paragraphs of text in books or on screen.

● Teach children how to complete **KWL** charts. At their simplest these record:
  ● What I already **K**now.
  ● What I **W**ant to know.
  ● What I **L**earned.

Additional columns can be added in to record, for example: 'Where I will look for information'. These charts will provide a framework for research and help children to define their questions. Once you have introduced a topic, let children begin to ask questions. (Be sure that you comply with the school's sex education policy). Teach children how to find out answers to their questions using all the media available.

● Have a Question Wall in the classroom where children can record questions on sticky notes. Others can find answers and write them on an adjacent sticky note. Challenge the children to write a related question each time they find the answer to a question already posted.

● Let children use ICT to create text to enshrine the information that they have discovered. Help them to hyperlink their work to other children's. They will need to read their peers' work carefully to decide where hyperlinks should go.

You Can... **Find out about games and sports**

Part of being healthy is keeping fit. Make the most of opportunities for exercise at school. Use reading as a way into learning more about games to play in the playground, more about sports and more about keeping healthy.

Thinking points

- In addition to the activities described above, you might like to introduce Brain Gym (www.braingym.org.uk/). There is significant research that shows physical activity, particularly when it involves both sides of the body and brain, helps to get children into a good frame of mind for learning.

- Research also suggests that children's concentration spans are about the same length as their age plus two in minutes so a 6-year-old child can concentrate for about eight minutes. After this amount of time, children will benefit from a short brain break. After a maximum of twice their age in minutes, children generally need some kind of physical activity.

Links to PE

EYFS and QCA:

- EYFS, PD: activities described on this page will support PD insofar as the reading always leads to and results from a physical activity. Through physical activities, children develop the knowledge and skills to play co-operative games as well as having opportunities to try and to learn.

- All Key Stage 1 units based on dance, gymnastics and invasion games will provide ideal links with these activities. Through linking the reading activities with PE, children can recognise the importance of reading for understanding instructions and navigating to websites or book pages.

Tips, ideas and activities

- Go orienteering:
  - Take photographs of places around the school.
  - Place an A5 letter or word at the place after you've taken the photograph. Tie it on or weigh it down so it can't be blown away.
  - Give each group of children a set of photographs.
  - Challenge them to run around the school and find the places shown in the photographs. They should write the letter or word they find on the back of each photograph.
  - Set a time limit on the activity that requires the children to move at a reasonable, but safe, pace.
  - When they get back to the classroom, ask them to use the letters or words to make a word or sentence.

- Follow links on the Teacher Resource Exchange (www.tre.ngfl.gov.uk) to find video clips of PE lessons. Follow them together on the whiteboard. Alternatively, go to BoogieBeebies (www.bbc.co.uk/cbeebies/boogiebeebies). Let children see you reading the links to navigate to the websites.

- Carry out a survey of games the children play in the playground. Ask them to tell you about the games they play. Categorise the games into imaginary games, chasing games, skipping games, and so on. If there are children who don't play games at playtimes, use circle time activities to find out whether this is from choice or not.

- Find out about playground games. Go to websites such as www.playgroundfun.org.uk to find instructions and rules for playing games, together with teaching materials. Some school websites (for example: www.woodlands-junior.kent.sch.uk/studentssite/playgroundgames.htm) also give instructions for playground games, often written by the children.

- Use the games you have read about as models for children to write their own instructions or rules for playing favourite games. This could involve sequencing photographs, either onscreen or on paper, with brief captions, or by writing longer instructions.

You Can... Become a Reading Champion

The Reading Champions Project is a nationwide scheme supported by the National Literacy Trust. The project arose in response to national concern about boys' reading and aims to identify and nurture positive male role models for reading. – not simply famous names, but men and boys who read for themselves and for other people. Find out more at: www.readingchampions.org.uk.

Thinking points

● The Reading Champions campaign is aimed at boys and men, but as an inclusive school you will want girls to engage too: they may need their own program.

● Contact sporting celebrities through their clubs. For actors' agents search *Spotlight* (www. spotlightcd.com): 'Who's Who' is also an excellent source for agents or contact addresses.

● Don't lose sight of the fact that you may have very good role models in your own school. As well as the classroom and teaching staff, consider caretakers, midday supervisors and road crossing patrol staff.

Reading Champions

There are many reasons for joining the Reading Champions campaign:

● it doesn't cost anything to join

● ideas and expertise can be shared within a national network

● the organisers will provide flexible support frameworks suited to your specific and regional requirements.

● excellent resources, posters, incentives and rewards are provided along with inspirational case studies

For more information see: www. literacytrust.org.uk/campaign/ Champions/about.html

Tips, ideas and activities

● Talk to the children about who their role models are and who they most want to be like when they grow up. Encourage children to think of named people outside of their families as well as family members. In groups, let them discuss why these are the people they want to be like.

● Give children the opportunity to research the named individuals who they wish to emulate. They will probably need internet access to do this. Ask the children to make short presentations to their groups, explaining what they have found out about their named person.

● If children have found an address for their named person, suggest that they could write a letter explaining why they so admire them.

● Use any sporting or television hero as a link into the Reading Champions campaign.

● Is there a professional or semi-professional sports club near you? It could be a football, rugby, tennis, cricket, hockey, netball or swimming club. Write to the club and ask if any of its members would come and talk to or read with the children as part of the Reading Champions campaign. The bigger football clubs often have an education division who will send top players out to visit schools.

● If any of the role models are not sports people, they can still be Reading Champions. It is still worth contacting them and asking if they are willing to come into school and talk to the children about their lives and interests.

● Whether you have visitors in school or not, emphasise to the children that champions, in all walks of life, read. If they want to be champions at anything, first they need to learn to read.

Ages
4–7

You Can... Create imaginary worlds

Reading gives children access to worlds that are quite different from their own. These worlds enrich the imagination and help children to explore their own sense of self. Picture books are the ideal portal into these other worlds where animals talk, magic is real and anything can happen.

Thinking points

● Fantasy stories and settings for young children can be broadly divided into two groups: those set in this world, but extraordinary things happen; and those set in an imaginary world. For the purposes of working with young children imaginary worlds can include jungles, under-water settings, volcanoes and dinosaur-inhabited swamps.

● Fantasy worlds are often a very safe place for children to explore PHSE ideas. They can recognise that characters in these worlds have feelings too, but 'hurts' can be mended more quickly than in real life.

Links to art and music

EYFS and QCA:

● EYFS, CD: the activities described on this page are all within the word and the spirit of the CD area of learning. By valuing children's imaginary worlds – no matter how bizarre or conventional – and giving them starters to help them to invent worlds, we can begin to harness the creativity that is essential to underpin learning.

● Art, Units 1B and 2B: establish materials available in this world.

● Music: explore rhythms, pitches and timbres, to create sound scenes in imaginary worlds.

Tips, ideas and activities

● Read to your children. Have a class focus on imaginary worlds and read stories and poems that are outrageous, funny, exciting, adventurous, beautiful, and so on.

● Cover mini-themes and tell the children that this week you are going to read books that are:
  ● Set in space or on weird planets.
  ● Set under the sea or in jungles.
  ● Set in a world like ours but where funny things happen.
Through the explicit introduction of these mini-themes you can introduce children to different types of fantasy story and poems.

● Develop phonics activities around the setting you have chosen, in which you can invent silly words and segment them to spell using your own choice of graphemes. In this world, children can't make the wrong choice, because there is no right choice.

● Make up silly rhymes (*The phlans go zop and the flomes will gop*) for the children to read and illustrate. Ask them to write subsequent rhymes to create a class nonsense poem.

● Transform your role-play corner into an imaginary setting using drapes, coloured foils and crepe paper. What kinds of artefacts will you need in this setting? What kinds of jobs might people do there? What will they need do to their jobs? Base your settings on books you have read and enjoyed.

● Play music while children explore different effects in art activities. How do different children respond to the music? What kinds of imaginary worlds are created to different musical tracks? Ask children to create a music track while you read a story to them.

● Use role play, based on stories you have shared, to develop ideas in the music- and art-inspired imaginary worlds. *What happens in these worlds? How do people/ creatures/ behave?*

You Can... **Explore imaginary worlds**

Reading is a window into other worlds. As children's reading improves, they will encounter more details about settings. Help them to explore how these details are built up and established by experienced writers who rarely write whole paragraphs of description, but drop in critical observations instead. In order that they can become skilful writers and engaged readers themselves, children need to develop a rich vocabulary of adjectives and adverbs.

Thinking points
● Discuss with the children why they think authors set their stories in imaginary worlds. Develop a discussion around the kinds of stories that are likely to be set in imaginary worlds.

● Develop the link between fantasy worlds as created in different media: art, drama, dance and music.

● Go on an e-visit to an art gallery (for example: www.nationalgallery. org.uk or www.tate.org.uk). Look at the way artists create imaginary worlds and compare it to the way that authors do. Ask different children to write a description of a different painting. The class can then try to match paintings and descriptions.

Recommended websites
● Listen to different types of music tracks from modern experimentalist composers. Try visiting www.soundclick.com or www.redferret.net, both of which have free and legal extracts from soundtracks so you can sample a wide variety of music.

● Show pictures of modern art. Use a search engine to find suitable sites, such as www.moma.org and then search around the sites to find art for the children to respond to, and to justify and explain their response.

Tips, ideas and activities
● Read to your children. Focus on imaginary worlds and read stories and poems that are outrageous, funny, exciting, adventurous, beautiful, and so on.

● 21st century children are used to observing rather than feeling. Find activities to extend children's vocabulary of texture, smell, taste and sound as well as sight. All of these activities will enrich reading experiences because you or the children need to read in order to access them.

● As children's vocabulary grows, read to them from established writers whose descriptive language is rich and flowing. Invite children to close their eyes while you read and to imagine themselves in the setting.

● Create a display that is a paint palette of light and dark colours. On top of each colour, write some adjectives and adverbs that are evoked by it. Ask children to write a description of a place using words from the dark side of the palette; then write a description of the same place using words from the light side. Children can read their descriptions to each other. Listeners should evaluate the success with which the author changes the mood of the text by using different vocabulary sets.

● Ask children to look out for well-created settings in their own reading. Make time available for children to read from their books and to explain why the setting is so successful.

● Let children respond to descriptions of settings through art or dance. They can establish more details about the setting either through showing its mood, or describing how movement occurs within it.

● Challenge children to create settings through imagery rather than straight description. Look out for imagery in books. Use similes and metaphors to describe pictures and sounds. Can children use them in their own writing?

You Can... **Find out about other countries**

Many young children find it hard to understand that people can have experiences that are different from their own. Since children are used to meeting unfamiliar ideas and landscape in stories, it is worth developing themes in stories to help children understand something about the cultures within which the stories are set. With a few stories, some simple non-fiction books and maybe a map, you can help even the youngest children to recognise and value different experiences.

Thinking points

● Before beginning any topic involving 'other people', it is worth spending some time exploring the children's prior knowledge Hearing about each others' lives can help children to recognise that they all have different life experiences.

● Travel agencies are often willing to help out if you ask them for information about a new country.

● Take the children on a virtual journey to the new country. Sit them in a bus or aeroplane style seating arrangement making sure that they are strapped safely into their seats. On the journey, begin to tell children some of the things they will experience when you arrive.

Links to geography
EYFS:

● EYFS, KUW: discussions around the activities suggested here can encourage skills such as observation, problem solving, prediction, and critical thinking. Although children may not be able to have first-hand experiences of being in other places, video and stories can help them to begin to imagine what it might be like to live somewhere else.

● Years 1 and 2: as children begin to look beyond their immediate environment, they can learn how reading about the places they are studying can help them.

Tips, ideas and activities

● Read stories from other countries. Once you have read a story, talk about what you can find out about the other country from it. You could consider:
  - Clothes: look at the pictures and use any reference to clothing in the text. *Are there any particular reasons for the characters to wear these clothes?*
  - Houses: search the pictures for buildings, both inside and out. *Are the houses similar to those near where you live? What's the same and what's different? Why might this be?*
  - Environment: *is there any reference, either in the text or the pictures, to the built or natural environment? Are there creatures in the story that you don't find at home?*
  - Events: *does the setting have any impact on the events in the story, or could they have happened in exactly the same way at home?* Explore how the setting impacts on events in a story.

● Use atlases, globes and maps to find out more about other countries. When you have found out where they are, use books, magazines, video and the internet to find out more about them. For example, visit:
  - www.recap.ltd.uk/podcasting to find examples of podcasts, often produced by or involving children, that will tell you more about communities around the world;
  - www.scottish-island-shopping.com/coll/vtour to find a virtual tour of Katie Morag's real home;
  - www.kids.nationalgeographic.com for images and video from National Geographic;
  - www.bbc.co.uk/cbbcnews to watch videos of places that have recently been in the news;
  - www.bbc.co.uk/schools/barnabybear for videos and images of Barnaby Bear in different places around the country and the world.

● Ask children who have been to a different location in this country, or abroad on holiday, to bring photographs and postcards and to prepare to talk about their experiences.

You Can... Find out about other countries

For some children, travelling the world is commonplace; for others a bus journey into a city is an adventure. At the time of year when so many are planning a summer break, it's good to find out more about places around the world.

Thinking points

- Read stories from, and about, countries you explore in geography. When they are finding out about countries, children are often as interested in the social geography as in the physical and political approach. Understanding the people will help children to gain a much better appreciation of the country.

- Use the children's own travel experiences as the basis for 'hot-seating' activities. All of the children can research the country to find questions and if the child in the 'hot-seat' doesn't know the answers, the questions can form the basis for later class research.

- The number of resources available for free grows all the time – but try to direct children to certain websites rather than letting them roam among websites designed for holiday makers.

Links to geography

- Throughout your work in geography, make sure that children are familiar with navigating the different sections in their reference book. Check that they know which books are organised alphabetically, which have a contents page or an index and how they are used.

- Make use of brightly coloured books and maps about different countries. These are particularly useful for non-English speaking and SEN children, since they are attractive and can give information through images as well as through the written word.

Tips, ideas and activities

- Read stories from other countries; include traditional tales as well as stories of everyday life which are set in other countries. Use the stories as springboards for discussion and exploration of other people's lives and cultures.

- Find people within the school community, or other visitors to invite into school, who have travelled and are willing to share their experiences with you. Ask the children to research information and prepare some questions beforehand.

- Use atlases, globes and maps to find out more about other countries. Visit www.oxfam.org.uk/education/resources/mapping_our_world for an amazing animation showing the globe flattening and tilting so you can see how countries physically relate to each other.

- When you have found out where countries are, use books, magazines, video and the internet to find out more about them and the people who live in them. For example visit:
  - www.bbc.co.uk/schools for a variety of animated activities;
  - www.bbc.co.uk/cbbcnews for places that have recently been in the news;
  - www.kids.nationalgeographic.com for images and videos from National Geographic.

- Use travel brochures to plan a holiday. Depending on the age of your children, you could give them certain parameters and ask them to act as your travel agent and find you a suitable holiday. Otherwise, let the children plan their own holiday and prepare to justify their choice.

- Let children earn country 'stamps' in a reading passport. Devise a generic country questionnaire (including, for example, continent, neighbouring countries or oceans, climate, rivers, population, language, currency, major cities, food and things and places the country is famous for.) Ask children to research a number of countries, finding out information as they go. When a child has researched a country, stamp their 'passport'.

You Can... Have a summer reading challenge

In an ideal world, young children would spend the long summer evenings playing outside – supervised, of course – learning to ride bicycles and skateboards, learning how to push themselves on a swing and learning how to enjoy imaginative play with each other. In the real word, however, many children stay indoors with a DVD or computer game. But if we can't make the children explore their own world, we should at least try to encourage them to explore the world of books.

Thinking points

- Before you publish your book list to parents, consider which books you are going to ask the children to read. You will need to work out how they are going to access the books in the summer holidays. Reading challenges are most successful when there are book lists available, since parents are more likely to encourage their children to join in.

- Check with the local library in advance of publishing your lists. They may be able to pull in stock from other libraries or suggest books of which they have multiple copies.

- Don't forget non-fiction books in your list.

Framework links

- Strands 1–4, speaking and listening: listening to stories, asking questions, retelling and discussing stories are key to developing speaking and listening skills.

- Strands 5–6, phonics and spelling: make sure that some of the books in your reading challenge are at an appropriate level for children to read by themselves. Help parents to understand how you use phonics to support reading.

- Strands 7–8, understanding, interpreting, engaging with and responding to texts.

Tips, ideas and activities

- Reading challenges work most effectively if the whole school takes part, although the challenge will need to be adapted for different classes. Use assemblies as well as class time to set up the challenges as well as to give rewards.

- Why not start now, or during the summer holidays, and cumulate with registering your school for the Readathon (www.readathon.org) during Children's Book Week in October?

- Discuss the idea of a reading challenge with the children. How many books is it reasonable for them to be expected to read? What kinds of books are they going to read? How much of each book must they read independently? Or are they allowed to have books read to them? You might consider having different categories of 'reading' in your challenge.

- How are you going to record success in your reading challenge? Different schools have evolved different systems, for example: writing each book on a 'leaf' and combining the leaves to make a reading bush; writing book names in shapes in a pattern, then colouring in the shape until all shapes are coloured; ticking book titles off a list; writing books read onto a list. You will need to agree a system with your class. There is no need for all classes to have the same system.

- Use school time to excite the children about the possibilities of their summer reading challenge: make a role-play corner into a story world; have a story-book characters parade (or announce one at the beginning of next term after the children have read their books); make pictures and friezes of favourite stories; share stories in assembly; invite an author or poet into school; ask the school cook to prepare a book-linked meal for the children.

You Can... **Have a summer reading challenge**

Begin a reading challenge now in order to create a momentum to carry children through a summer of reading. Although you hope that children are outdoors enjoying the light evenings, the reality is that many of them will experience periods of boredom during the summer evenings. By persuading them to read instead of watching television or playing computer games, you can help them to learn about creating imaginary worlds and losing themselves in a book.

Thinking points
● Book fairs are great starting points for reading challenges.

● Encourage the whole staff to be enthusiastic: why not run a reading challenge in the staffroom as well?

● Plan this term for the celebration in the autumn. How will you reward the children's reading – with stickers, certificates, an award evening? If you plan for this now, it will probably happen; if you don't, this year's challenge may fizzle out.

Now try this
● Contact your local library to warn them that you're having a reading challenge.

● Visit the National Literacy Trust website (www.literacytrust.org.uk) for up-to-date information about reading challenges and the National Year of Reading

● Use the School's Library Association website (www.sla.org.uk) for ideas.

● Visit Letterbox Library (www.letterboxlibrary.com) for lists of books for inclusion.

● Their Reading Futures (www.theirreadingfutures.org.uk) supports summer reading challenges as does The Reading Agency (www.readingagency.org.uk). If one is being run in your local library, you may want to join forces with them.

Tips, ideas and activities
● Your first challenge is to persuade all of your colleagues to take part in a whole school reading challenge. You can do it with just your class, but will their next teacher reward their efforts at the beginning of next term? A whole school challenge is by far the most effective.

● Your second challenge is to ensure that your reading challenge is inclusive. You know your school community, so you will know about involving all families whatever their culture, language or knowledge about reading. You will have to make decisions about which language you want the children to read in; you should ensure access arrangements for any child who needs assistive technology; you may also need to consider how to include traveller children and recent immigrants. Almost every school will also need to consider how to include their struggling readers. (Look at www.readingrockets.org/helping for some ideas.)

● Your third challenge is to motivate the children to read. Why not start by talking to the children about what motivates them? Start the ball rolling by giving them a list of ideas and asking groups of children to rank the ideas. Your list will vary depending on the age and maturity of the children you teach, but some ideas could be
- Making a list of 'Books I've read' and adding to it.
- Reading other children's book recommendations.
- Reading comics.
- Reading books suggested on a list.
- Reading anything I want to.
- Reading for a school research project.
- Reading everything by one author.
- Going to the library and browsing for books.
- Reading around a topic that interests me.
- Reading more books than anyone else.

● Your final challenge is to start the excitement now: build it up towards the end of term and celebrate it in the autumn.

You Can... Enjoy songs and rhymes

We have sung and recited rhymes to our babies and young children for centuries. The number of poetry collections and anthologies that are published each year are testament to the fact that we still enjoy sharing songs and rhymes with young children.

Thinking points

● It's worth finding and keeping your own favourite poetry anthology. Look for books that include the work of more than one poet; that have a variety of types and that include a range from simple to challenging.

● The Renewed Literacy Framework makes recommendations for poetry and rhyme, but give children experience of a far greater range. The Framework only recommends forms that children should work on; it doesn't intend to limit children's experience of poetry.

● Be prepared for strong reactions to some poems and rhymes. Children who have experienced emotional upheaval may be affected by particular poems or images.

Cross-curricular links

● Science: choose a theme of poetry linked to a KWL or science topic, find related rhymes and poems and let the children lead the learning to answer their own questions from the rhymes.

● History: find out about the origins of some of our traditional rhymes and teach them as part of a history topic. *London's Burning* is a clear example. Let the children ask questions arising from the poem and you'll find that many QCA learning objectives will be covered.

Tips, ideas and activities

● Teach children your favourite songs and rhymes. Talk about why you like them so much and see how quickly your children learn them.

● By all means buy tapes and CD-ROMs to sing along to, but also sing and recite yourself - the children won't mind if you are off-key! Most importantly, you can adapt the pace to cater for the speed of your children. Some children who sing only to CD-ROMs can become discouraged if they can't process or say the words quickly enough to keep up.

● Develop awareness of different modern poets, whose work is often more accessible for younger children. Include poets who write picture books as well as poets who write poems on one page. Repeat the poems often enough for the children to be able to join in. Even if they can't join in with the whole rhyme or poem, there may be a chorus or repeated line that they can enjoy. But don't forget the old favourites too – even five-year-olds can get goose bumps during a well performed *Tyger, Tyger, Burning Bright* by William Blake.

● Find CD-ROMs and videos of poets reading aloud from their own work. You can see and hear an enormous number for free at: www.poetryarchive.org/poetryarchive/listenPoetry.do or visit poets' own websites to see or hear them in action, for example: www.michaelrosen.co.uk.

● Teach children to become poetry critics, asking them to comment on different aspects of a poem that they particularly enjoy or dislike. Give them a number of things to talk about and let them present their responses to a variety of poems and rhymes:
  ● What is the poem about?
  ● What are the best words?
  ● Does the poem rhyme and does it matter?
  ● How does the poem make me feel?

You Can... Be positive about poetry

Teaching poetry to children in Key Stage 2 can be one of those life-affirming topics that make you realise how much you enjoy the job. Children are generally gripped either by the 'mechanics' of the rhythm and rhyme, or by the power and conciseness of the language. Harness that interest and teach poetry to make an impact on your children's learning.

Thinking points
● Buy CD-ROMs and videos of poets reading aloud from their own work. You can see and hear an enormous number for free at www.poetryarchive.org/poetryarchive/listenPoetry.do or visit poets' own websites to see or hear them in action.

● The Renewed Literacy Framework makes recommendations for poetry and rhyme, but give children experience of a far greater range. The Framework only recommends forms that children should work on; it doesn't intend to limit the scope of poems that the children experience.

● Ensure that you have a range of anthologies in your classroom and encourage children to read them. Be aware that many poems are written to be read aloud, so try to make provision for children to share poems by reading aloud.

Recommended websites
● www.poetry4kids.com: an American site with rhymes, activities and poetry challenges.

● www.poetry-online.org: a UK site that includes children's poems.

● www.storyit.com/Classics/JustPoems/classicpoems.htm: an American site with popular poems from the UK and in the US.

● www.love-poems.me.uk: a UK site with a comprehensive list of favourite children's poems including nursery rhymes.

Tips, ideas and activities
● Use a whole range of poems with your class. Most children will enjoy chanting some of the more accessible and often humorous modern verse; but also explore some of the poems you remember and enjoy, which may be more challenging, but are worth the investment of time and effort.

● Give your children poems, or verses of longer poems, to learn by heart. Have a weekly session during which children all recite from the poems they have learned. This can be very inclusive since even those who might have struggled to learn the poem properly can join in where they can in a whole class experience. Even if the recitation is mechanistic, children can still experience the rhythm and rhyme and hear the pattern of the language.

● Once children know a poem well, let them perform it. This gives all children the experience of finding meaning in text and considering how to use body language, gesture, facial expression and intonation to emphasise the meaning in the poem. For many children, this is a rare experience but a very powerful one in enhancing self-esteem.

● Explore different ways of extending the meaning of the poem. Too often, we teach children about the mechanics of poetry - and it's a valuable lesson in its own right - but celebrating the meaning is even more important. Can the children:
  ○ Write a sequel?
  ○ Think of alternative outcomes?
  ○ Write another poem in the style of…?
  ○ Take an image from the poem and extend or amend it?

● Talk about why a poet decided to write a poem rather than a story. The narrative poems of Michael Rosen are a good place to start this conversation (visit www.michaelrosen.co.uk to hear him performing one of them.) Help children to understand what drives a poet to be a poet.

You Can... **Teach reading skills through songs and rhymes**

Rhythm and rhyme are entirely fundamental to reading. There is significant research to suggest that awareness of rhyme in the early years is one of the most successful predictors of prowess in reading. Songs and rhymes are powerfully motivational for learners and great fun for teachers.

Thinking points

● Play games that focus on rhyme such as rhyming snap or bingo. At first use pictures, then progress to matching a picture to a rhyming word and finally to two rhyming words. As children get older, use different spelling patterns in the pairs of words (for example: *right*, *white*). These activities will reinforce a child's ability to recognise the patterns that are vital for English.

● Check at your local library for *Rhyme Time* sessions and advertise them to parents. These are free and are likely to have a slot especially for children aged between four and seven. These sessions will include poetry performances as well as activities for the children and parents to join in.

Links to Letters and Sounds, EYFS and the Framework

● Letters and Sounds: these activities are appropriate for children working within phases 1–6. Adapt the spelling and the rhymes to match your current phonics focus.

● EYFS, CLL: rhythm and rhyme are embedded in this area of learning, so any activity you do will be within the word and spirit of the EYFS.

● Key Stage 1: Poetry and rhyme is recommended for every year group and in most terms. Ideas and schemes of work can be found at www.standards.dfes.gov.uk.

Tips, ideas and activities

● Use rhythm and rhyme to teach useful lists. Many children learn to sing the alphabet (check that they know *l*, *m*, *n*, *o*, *p*), but also find songs, rhymes and rhythms to teach things such as days of the week, months and times tables.

● Teach finger rhymes. Although these are often seen as the preserve of younger children, many older children enjoy them too.

● For Year 1 and 2 children, use poems and rhymes as vehicles for teaching children about reading and reciting with expression, about fluency, about using the voice to create pace and tension. Recite Humpty Dumpty in a way to make the children laugh, sleep or feel angry. Talk about what you changed to influence their reactions. Let children experiment with using more advanced reading skills when reading these well-known texts.

● Many decodable texts are written in rhyme. Websites such as www.starfall.com/n/level-a/learn-to-read/load.htm include free decodable texts that you can use to practise decoding to read. Point out the patterns in words. Identify pairs of rhyming words and discuss how you would know that they rhyme.

● Play with substituting different rhyming words into familiar rhymes: Humpty Dumpty sat on *a box* or *chair*; Twinkle Twinkle little *light* or *moon*; Incy Wincy spider climbed up the *water pipe*. Can children edit the next lines to make them rhyme?

● Explore the syllable rhythm of animal names. Helping children to hear syllables is an important part of learning to listen to sounds in words. Young children need to begin to break up the stream of language into words and syllables; older ones need to be able to distinguish syllables to help them to read and write longer words successfully.

You Can... Develop reading skills through poetry and rhyme

Poetry and rhyme are great vehicles for developing children's understanding of the 'mechanics' of reading and writing through word and sentence level activities. It is crucial that children read poems mainly for enjoyment and to explore meaning – but they can also have fun with the mechanics of language.

Thinking points

● Although *Letters and Sounds* is intended for children working in Key Stage 1, many of the spelling objectives that used to be in Key Stage 2 are now included in it. You can find it online at www.standards. dfes.gov.uk/phonics.

● As far as possible, let children set the agenda for deciding what to explore in a poem. If you are intending to teach an objective from Strand 7 'Understanding and Interpreting Texts' of the Renewed Literacy Framework, share the objective with the children and then invite them to ask questions. If both the research questions and the exploration are initiated by the children, the learning will be more secure.

Framework links

● Poetry and rhyme is recommended for every year group and most terms. Visit www.standards.dfes.gov.uk/ primaryframeworks/literacy/ planning to find planning ideas and schemes of work.

● While you can use this planning guidance and the related objectives to identify particular types of poetry to use, the intention of the Framework is not to limit the types of poems that children can experience and enjoy. Make sharing poems something that happens on a regular basis.

Tips, ideas and activities

With all the ideas listed below, make links to poems that your class enjoy rather than using the examples shown.

● Use poems and rhymes to develop an understanding of spelling and spelling patterns. Give children copies of poems to read (differentiate the poems so that children read poems that are appropriate) and ask them to highlight rhyming words. They can then explore spelling patterns within those rhyming words. Are they the same? What are the variations? Which variation is more common?

● Explore scanning. The words scan and scansion have a very specific meaning in poetry when they are used to refer to the rhythm and number of syllables in a line of rhyming poetry – or in a Shakespeare play. Ask half of the children to clap the beat of a line of a familiar poem or rhyme while the other half clap the rhythm. Talk about how the precise choice of words in the poem must match the rhythm of a line in order to 'scan'. (For example, why might a poet sometimes refer to a character as Billy and sometimes as Bill?)

● Explore which words can swap order in a sentence without impacting on the meaning. For example, explore a line such as: '*A father Billy had*'. Discuss the more usual word order when writing prose: '*Billy had a father*'. How does the meaning change when the word order is altered? Which words in the sentence could change order? Could you have '*Billy father a had*'? What about if the words were changed to '*A father had a Billy*', why does that change the meaning? Use sentences from poems that you read together to explore word order and meaning.

● Once children have explored and investigated the words that the poet used, suggest that they focus on alternative words the poet might have used. How does that impact on the rhyme, scanning and sentence structure? For example, how would replacing the names of the characters in *Jack and Jill* with *Sridhar and Sinead* impact on the rhyme?

You Can... Develop confident readers through songs and rhymes

Attitude and confidence are intrinsic to reading success, particularly for four- to seven-year-olds. If you give your children the belief that they can read and the expectation that they will be able to make sense of a text, then they will be more robust when it comes to meeting the challenge of an unrecognised word. The beneficial impact of this should be continued as children grow.

Thinking points

● Parents sometimes complain that children are just reading from memory. This is fine as long as the children are behaving like readers. As children get older, you need to increase the challenge. The easiest way to discover whether they are using memory is to cover the text and ask them to recite it. If the lack of text makes no difference, they were relying on memory; if they get stuck, they were probably using memory to support reading.

● Beware of determining whether or not a child is reading words in singing lessons until you have worked with the child individually. Some children cannot read the words quickly enough; others may be able to follow the song without recognising individual words.

Recommended websites

These websites are useful to find resources or activities to promote shared, guided or independent reading:

● www.woodlands-junior.kent.sch.uk

● www.crickweb.co.uk/Key-Stage-1.html

● www.teachingideas.co.uk/earlyyears/contents.htm

● www.ngfl-cymru.org.uk/vtc-home/vtc-ey-home/vtc-ey-llcs

● www.learninggrids.com

● www.sparklebox.co.uk

Tips, ideas and activities

● Find, or make, interactive whiteboard screens of songs, poems and rhymes to read with your children. Ask children to point to words as they read: can they identify individual words? If you mask a word, can they predict it from context?

● Give children words to read and follow when you teach them new songs to sing in music and assemblies. Ideally, let children have paper copies of songs because tracking back and forth on a vertical screen at the front of a hall is tricky for emerging readers. If you can't give children individual copies, make use of colour on the screen the children are reading from so that they can tell which line they are on and see where to go next. Children often learn songs very quickly because they have the tune as well as the rhythm to give them clues.

● Create 'rebus' rhymes using images from clip art programmes. Rebus texts have a mixture of decodable words and images for the tricky words. So, for the line '*If you should meet a crocodile*'. The word *crocodile* would be replaced by an image of a crocodile. Rebus texts are comparatively easy to construct and are very supportive in encouraging children to read since they can enjoy the 'puzzle' aspect, which can detract from any anxieties as well as enabling you to share poems and rhymes with a more challenging vocabulary.

● Make a class book of familiar rhymes. Look at picture books of rhymes and talk about how each line, or pair of lines, is illustrated. Challenge children to provide illustrations to make their own rhyme picture book. Illustrating a rhyme makes the child read the line and demonstrate understanding.

You Can... # Develop children's self-esteem using poetry and rhyme

Poetry and rhyme can be a lifeline for many struggling or reluctant readers in Key Stage 2. By the time these children have 'failed' to learn to read successfully for three years, they often 'know' they can't read and will reject the idea of themselves as readers. Try using poems and rhymes as a 'way in' for these children.

Thinking points

● Poems with set rhythms and rhymes are often useful for giving to struggling readers. Try limericks and poems with little rhyming couplets.

● Many suitable poems will be in anthologies for younger children, so type them out with spaces and ask children to draw illustrations. This gives them ownership of the rhymes as well as testing their comprehension of the poem.

● Try jokes and riddles. They are often very accessible while having high status among the class.

Links to Letters and Sounds

Although it is written for Key Stage 1 teachers, *Letters and Sounds* (www.standards.dfes.gov.uk/local/clld/las.html) can help you to cater for Key Stage 2 children who are not making appropriate progress in reading. It divides the teaching of phonics into six phases. Its key concepts are:

● Children should be taught to 'segment to spell': to orally sound words out, phoneme by phoneme, and count how many phonemes are in the word.

● Children should be taught to 'blend to read': to sound words out in their reading; they shouldn't be asked to read words that feature graphemes (letter patterns) with which they aren't yet familiar.

Tips, ideas and activities

What do you think are the virtues of poems as texts for reluctant readers? Having identified your own top ten virtues for children in your class, exploit those features and support your children. Here are some ideas to start you thinking:

● Begin by looking for short poems. Unlike reading books, which tend to be levelled, poems cannot be grouped in this way because some of the most complex and concise poems are much more challenging than some longer easy poems. For struggling readers, brevity and ease combine to make a non-threatening text. If higher attaining readers are also reading short poems, then your struggling readers don't look as if they are reading anything that is different from the rest of the class.

● Search for poems with a fairly decodable text. Current thinking suggests that phonics should be taught as children's first strategy for reading unrecognised words. Assuming that you are continuing to teach phonics to these children, try to find poems that feature the current phonics focus. Increasingly, poets are writing for a younger audience and many are aiming to use more decodable words. Just because you find the poem in a book with illustrations for younger children, doesn't mean that you have to give it to your older readers in that form.

● Look for poems with rhyme and rhythm. Both of these features give great clues for a child who is trying to make an 'educated guess' at a word, since a lot of words are ruled out because they wouldn't fit. Moreover, if you read the poem aloud first, then the rhyme and the rhythm will provide additional clues for children to use memory as an aide to reading the poem.

● Find age-appropriate funny poems. Most of your class will probably appreciate funny poems and if your struggling readers are able to read, recite and remember some, they will gain status in the eyes of their peers.

You Can... # Find out about holiday sports and activities

What are the children in your class going to do during the summer holidays? Having a reading challenge is one thing, but why not find out before the end of term about activities in your local area and enthusing the children about the possibility of attending? Most local authorities provide some level of financial support.

Thinking points

● While you are encouraging your children to plan for their summer holidays, you might want to think about your own. Hopefully, you will have organised some time to wind down and recharge your batteries. It is important for your wellbeing.

● In addition to your down-time, what other activities have you planned? Yes, there will be planning to do, books to label, the academic year ahead to organise but you should also be thinking about some kind of physical activity to keep your body working even while your mind is resting. Decorating the house might work for some people but for others it might be gardening, walking, running, swimming or dance classes! The summer holiday is the ideal time to start participating in a physical activity you have always wondered about. Go on, give yourself a break. Begin a new physical activity to keep your body and mind healthy both for the holidays and for the new academic year.

Recommended websites

See page 31 for a list of websites that you can use to find resources or activities to promote shared, guided or independent reading, including rhymes and poems.

Tips, ideas and activities

● Contact local leisure centres, swimming pools, tennis clubs, dance studios and amateur dramatic organisations: ask them to send your school details of activities for children of the age you teach. Search online and in local directories for those that might appeal to a broad range of interests.

● If there is a local holiday club, contact it and find out what it has to offer for your children. Many run for just part of the holiday, others are Ofsted registered and run all year round.

● Once you have a range of brochures and activity types, let the children browse them and decide what they might enjoy doing. Most of these brochures will not be written for your children to read, so encourage children to make use of any strategies they can to make meaning from the brochure. There may be pictures, web-links that children can follow, or children may just be able to comment on the presentation of the leaflet to decide whether it looks attractive and makes them want to find out more.

● Use one of the brochures for shared or guided reading sessions in which you discuss strategies for making meaning from this kind of text. If the children have strong opinions about the leaflet, encourage them to write to its producers, expressing their opinions. Customer feedback should always be valued by the organisation!

● Make a class list of all the activities that might be interesting to the children. Write relevant details on the list, including dates, price and venue. Print the list out and encourage children to find and highlight the activities that they think sound particularly interesting. You may want to limit the number they can highlight! Encourage children to take the list home so that parents know what the whole class and their child in particular, are interested in.

You Can... **Keep up to date with your team**

School's out. The long summer holidays are here. So how can you make sure that your children keep reading? Reading challenges can be powerful motivators, but children should also be using their reading as part of their day-to-day lives. During the holidays, they have time to engage more with the media to find out about the progress of their team – be it cricket, tennis, swimming, judo or any other team they follow.

Thinking points

● While the children are getting enthused with sports and activities, what are you planning to do… after that 'winding down' period that you so richly deserve? Does your local gym or sports club run holiday sessions for adults? Your physical and mental wellbeing is as important as that of your class and summer is often the time of year when you have the time to consider any lifestyle changes you might want to make.

● When the flyer comes through your door advertising all the evening classes in the local college that start in September, don't consign it to the recycling bin immediately without looking at possibilities for exercise for yourself. If aerobics, spinning, kick-boxing and training for half-marathons isn't what you want, look out for line dancing, salsa, Pilates, yoga or synchronised swimming classes!

Recommended websites

Some useful websites for finding out about sporting events, or different kinds of sport are listed below:

● www.bbc.co.uk/sport

● www.skysports.com

● www.olympics.org.uk

● www.sportengland.org

Tips, ideas and activities

● Before the end of the summer term, talk to your class about their involvement in any kind of sport outside of school. Involvement can include actively taking part, or following and supporting a team. Ask the children to make Venn diagrams to show how they are involved in sport.

● List all of the ways that children know of keeping abreast of events in their sport. Include print media (for example: magazines, newspapers, flyers and adverts) as well as ICT (for example: television, radio, texts and the internet). If the children have any sporting activities planned in the holidays, are they likely to receive certificates, medals, trophies or any other memorabilia of the event?

● Before the holidays, ask children to bring in printed examples – if they can – of each of the media. Discuss the kind of information you can get from each and evaluate its use for different purposes and different audiences.

● Talk about how children might complete a 'sports record' of their sports experiences during the holiday. This could take a number of different forms, for example:

- Digital camera images of them involved in their sports, together with captions so that the images are put in context and will have a meaning at some time in the future or for a different audience.
- Certificates and pictures of medals/trophies. These will also need extended captions for different times and audiences, explaining what was done to achieve the award. This could be accompanied by leaflets if available, advertising or explaining what the activity is about.
- A cuttings diary showing the progress of their team. This could include cuttings from magazines or newspapers, or printed pages from the internet.

You Can... **Organise an Olympics**

What do your children know about the Olympics? They may remember in August 2008, some of their favourite television programmes were replaced by the Olympics and they may have seen coverage on the build up to the London Olympics in 2012. The more children know and understand about the games, the more likely they are to take an interest. Do some brief research into the Olympics, then organise your own Olympics in school.

Thinking points

● One of the most important parts of organising an Olympic games is competing with the Olympic spirit. Ensure that all of the children understand that taking part and representing your class or team is as important as winning. The Olympic ideal is not that competitors cheat or winners boast too much or those who don't win burst into tears.

● Trying to teach the Olympic ideal to four- to seven-year-olds is tricky. You might want to model it in class, preferably with an adult accomplice with whom you can discuss losing at board games. Boost the spirits of the children who don't win by congratulating them on their Olympic spirit.

Recommended websites

These websites have information and ideas that you can use to help children to understand and engage with the Olympic Games.

● www.london2012.com – Official website of the London Olympic Games.

● www.olympics.org.uk – British Olympic Association.

● www.first-school.ws/activities/firststeps/olympics.htm

● www.npl.org/pages/KidsPlace/Sites/olympics.html

● www.atozkidsstuff.com/oly.html

Tips, ideas and activities

● Ask your children what they know or have heard about the Olympic Games. Summarise their understanding in a list.

● Display the CBBC Newsround sports web page http://news.bbc.co.uk/cbbcnews/hi/sport on an interactive whiteboard and browse for information on the Olympics to give children some understanding of the history of the games.

● Show the children the official Olympic website at www.olympic.org to find out about the Olympic spirit and the symbolism of the five rings.

● Together, visit other sites such as those listed below to find lists of sports, together with dates and venues of the competition.

● Talk about what an Olympics might look like in school. *Which sports or activities would it involve? Where could it take place? Would it have to be all on one day, or could it be spread out over several days?*

● *What would the rewards be? Would you have both individual and team awards (as the Olympics has, with individual and country awards)? What will the rewards look like? Real medals, certificates, applause?*

● Ask groups of children to consider these questions and to put together an 'Olympic bid'. This could be in any medium including drawing, cutting out pictures to make a collage, writing or using the computer. The idea is for children to engage with the principle of organising an event and to use the class research as the basis for their work.

● Combine the best features of the children's Olympic bids and make an official bid to the leadership team. It may be that only one class is taking part, or you may open the bidding structure to more than one class, but ensure that all children and classes who are interested are included.

● Good luck with your Olympic games!

You Can... **Find out about the Olympics**

The London Olympics take place from 27 July–12 August 2012. The approach to take when teaching about the Olympics will depend on other projects you are doing in school, but as a one-off day at the end of term, try one of these activities to whet your children's appetite and encourage them to take some interest in this spectacle.

Thinking points

● These activities are not true 'Mantle of the Expert' activities because there is not room to explain them properly so they are not sufficiently well structured. They do, however, capture the essence of a 'Mantle' activity and might be an interesting starting point for you and your class. For more information on 'Mantle of the Expert' go to www.mantleoftheexpert.com.

● This activity assumes that the children know a little about the Olympics. Use the sites below but also look at the activities on page 35.

● Do the children know where other Olympics have taken place? Help them to find out more about the different cities and their history.

Recommended websites

● www.london2012.com – Official website of the London Olympic Games.

● www.olympics.org.uk – British Olympic Association.

● www.visitolympics.co.uk – an unofficial blog, but with lots of information.

● www.olympicvideogames.com – this website will become more active with official video footage as the games start.

Tips, ideas and activities

Try some 'Mantle of the Expert' type activities where you give children the opportunity of assuming the role of expert and of researching the information they need for that role.

● Ask children to take on the expert role of travel agent booking you a holiday to enjoy the Olympics. Divide the children into groups and challenge each group to come up with the best holiday package they can for you.

○ Decide how you want the children to research the activity. Are they going to use travel brochures (in which case you will need to visit your travel agent) or the internet?

○ Begin by describing your travelling needs: how many people are in your party, how long you want to stay, particular attractions you need to see and your budget.

○ Give all of the children the same information and see what they come up with. Ask each group to make a presentation at the end of the day, explaining their response to your requirements. Tell the children which holiday you would book and explain why.

● Ask the children to take on the expert role of Olympic reporters. They can work in pairs or alone.

○ Each child/pair needs to choose an Olympic sport that they want to follow.

○ Children should research their sport, finding out who the members of their national team are and who the medal contenders from other countries are.

○ At the end of the day, let groups of children do a short presentation to other members of their group. The presentations should describe the research and make medal predictions.

○ Each group should nominate one presentation for the whole class to hear and enjoy.

You Can... Turn children into readers

One of the most important factors in learning to read is learning to love reading. All young children have the right to learn to read and to learn to love books and reading. The challenge for us is how to help them when there is so much competition from more visual media.

Thinking points

● Young children are quick to pick up on their teacher's enthusiasms; so if you establish reading as a high-value subject, you will influence your children to enjoy reading.

● Bring in your favourite book, having prepared a brief presentation on it, and tell the children why you like it.

Reading targets

P-scale and National Curriculum Reading attainment targets:

● **P5** Pupils show curiosity about content at a simple level, for example, they may answer basic two key-word questions about a story.

● **P7** Pupils show an interest in the activity of reading.

● **1B** Pupils respond to events and ideas in poems, stories and non-fiction.

● **2A** Pupils express opinions about events and actions and comment on some of the ways in which the text is written or presented.

● **2C** Pupils show understanding of texts, recount the main events or facts with support and comment on obvious features of the text, for example, good / bad characters.

● **3** In responding to fiction and non-fiction, pupils show understanding of the main points and express preferences.

Tips, ideas and activities

● Make sure that your daily class read is never driven out by other curriculum demands. If something has to go, choose something else and make reading a high priority.

● Have an attractive book corner in your classroom. Include displays of themed books linked either to a topic or to an author/ illustrator. Fewer books, rotated regularly and displayed well is better than a crammed bookshelf.

● Try to include relaxing seating in your book corner so that children feel that it is an enticing and important part of their classroom.

● Make time for children to browse the books and activities in your book corner. If possible, spend some time there with them, reading, sharing and talking about books.

● Give children shoe boxes for 'book box show and tell'. Ask children to put in the shoebox a favourite book together with items they make, write, draw or collect that are related to the book. The books can include non-fiction books, stories, fairy tales, nursery rhymes, poems, alphabet books and even catalogues if they might be a way into reading for some children. Allow children time to talk about their 'book boxes'.

● Encourage children to develop favourite authors and illustrators. Let them talk to the class about why a particular author or illustrator appeals to them.

● Ask children to write or draw a brief recommendation about a book that they have read. Let them share the book with the class, then display the book and recommendation in your book corner.

You Can... **Turn children into readers**

All children have the right to learn to love reading: our challenge is to give them the opportunities and to convince them that reading is 'cool'. Children are bombarded with information and ideas through multimedia, so most children are literate to some degree. But how can we turn them into passionate readers?

Thinking points

- Children in primary schools are often influenced by what their teacher likes, so if you enjoy reading they will generally try to enjoy it too. Treat them as equals as you describe your reading journeys to them.

- When you talk to the children about your own reading, use the familiar language of genres. If you enjoy crime fiction, romantic fiction or historical fiction, talk to the children about why. You probably use genre, as a well as author, as a filter to select your next book, so share this strategy with the children.

Recommended websites

- Information about organising an author to come and visit you in school: www.writingtogether.org.uk

- Publishers' websites that have author biographies include: www.bloomsbury.com and www.orchardbooks.co.uk/links.htm (this gives links to individual authors' and illustrators' websites.)

- The Internet School Library Media Centre (ISLMC) has links to a wide variety of authors' and illustrators' websites: http://falcon.jmu.edu/~ramseyil/biochildhome.htm

Tips, ideas and activities

- Make sure that your daily class read is never driven out by other curriculum demands. If something has to go, choose something else and make reading to and with your children a high priority.

- Choose class novels that are exciting, engaging, vivid and just above the general level of reading attainment of your children. Try to match the novels to meet the needs and interests of different classes.

- Make your class library into an attractive and high-profile part of the classroom. Rotate the books regularly so that there is always something new and interesting to read.

- Teaching children to select books is an important part of helping them to become readers. Include a selection of 'easy reads' that are available to all children but also include books that are appropriate for the struggling reader. Arrange fiction books by genre rather than alphabetically and try to make sure that there are appropriate picture books included in each section. Use an appropriate classification system for your non-fiction books.

- Talk about authors and illustrators. If you can't invite one to come and visit the class, find videos and biographies of them on the internet.

- Invite children to respond to and recommend books in a wide variety of ways. These can include: a presentation, talking about the book; a written recommendation for display; a role play with friends to explore themes in the book; a PowerPoint® presentation to develop topics, particularly in non-fiction; a recording of a poem performance; a picture or collage of a scene from the book. Encourage the children to decide on the most appropriate response to a book of their choice.

You Can... **Explore different cultures**

Where do the children in your class come from? Do you have books, poems and stories from all of the cultures? Give all of your children, including those who are from the UK, the chance to explore their cultural identities through books and reading.

Thinking points

● Consider your reading books from the point of view of a child whose culture isn't English. Do these children receive enough variety and insights into their own cultures? It isn't possible to write a reading scheme to meet the needs of every individual in the class, but using a variety of schemes gives different children the opportunity to relate with particular characters and cultures.

● What have you learned about your culture from books? How did you learn it? Why do you remember it? Use your own experience as a springboard for helping children to develop cultural identify from books.

● Make use of your school library service and local library. Both will have a range of books from different cultures and will be happy to help you to find appropriate picture books for your class.

Links to EYFS and SEAL

EYFS, KUW: 'communities' is one of the key aspects of KUW and is about how children begin to know about their own and other people's cultures in order to understand and celebrate the similarities and differences between them in a diverse society.

Key Stage 1: this work links well to SEAL pack theme 1: New Beginnings, as it gives you, individual children and your class a chance to explore your individual and collective identities.

Tips, ideas and activities

● Update your classroom library. There are many picture books now available that celebrate different cultures. Even if you don't have children from other cultures in your class, your class library should include books from different cultures showing positive images. Subscribe to a magazine such as Child Education Plus (http://magazines.scholastic.co.uk) or Books for Keeps (www.booksforkeeps.co.uk) that reviews picture books and makes a particular point of celebrating diversity.

● Use specialist bookshops such as Letterbox Library (www.letterboxlibrary.com) or Norfolk Children's Book Centre (www.ncbc.co.uk) to order, find or discuss books for your school library.

● Invite other members of staff and parents to come to the class with picture books that they particularly enjoy. These can be in any language or from any culture. Ask the adults to read and talk about the book including what it means to them. Let children explore the pictures and find out what they can about the characters and setting.

● Teach children to ask questions and 'interrogate a text' to find out about characters and setting. Just looking at the pictures will often give rise to questions: there might be unusual buildings, crops, even colours used in the illustration. Look at what the people in the picture backgrounds are doing and think about why they are busy, what the outcome of their action might be and what this tells us about the people and the place.

● Look at how the characters speak to each other. Do they speak in the same way children speak to each other in the classroom? Look too at how the characters are dressed. Are they dressed as children are in the classroom?

● By teaching children to 'interrogate a text', including pictures, they can find out a lot about their own and other cultures without needing to be able to read an entire book.

You Can... Find out about different cultures

Whether or not you have children from different cultures in your classroom, children today are growing up in a world where they need to know about, and respect, other cultures and people. In many parts of the UK, that understanding needs to extend into Eastern Europe and travelling communities as well as the more settled cultural communities. The starting point for an understanding of other cultures must be to understand their own cultural values and those of their friends in order that they can begin to appreciate why others' cultural values are so important to them.

Thinking points

● Browse through the books to ensure that you have a wide variety of cultures represented and not just people with different skin tones. If you need advice on acquiring new books, ask your school library service, the local library or specialist booksellers.

● Even if all the children in your class are white British, find out about the cultural differences between them (consider church/chapel membership; diet; time spent in the area)

● Use the internet to talk to children in other schools and share your research with them.

SEAL links

This work links well to SEAL pack theme 1: New Beginnings as it gives you, individual children and your class a chance to explore your individual and collective identities.

1b) to recognise their worth as individuals, by identifying positive things about themselves and their achievements, seeing their mistakes, making amends and setting personal goals

2e) to reflect on spiritual, moral, social and cultural issues, using imagination to understand other people's experiences.

Tips, ideas and activities

● Ask children to work in groups to talk about their own homes and families. Each group should make a list of similarities and differences in their experiences in the home. You may find it useful to give children a list of things to discuss in order to start their discussions. A list could include, for example: *which family members do you see every week? Do you observe any religious practices? What kind of clothes do you wear at the weekend? If you have to go to a special event, what kind of clothes do you wear? What kind of food do you eat at home? Are there any foods you will never eat? Who is the 'boss' in your house? What is the most important thing for you outside school?* Depending on your relationship with the children in your class, you can also ask other, more searching questions that you know might be interesting and informative in your class.

● Collate the children's answers into a class response and together read and evaluate the list. *Are there any surprising findings?* Is it the case, for example, that some children who were assumed to come from similar cultures actually live very different lives?

● Give pairs or small groups of children the task of researching more into a culture that is not their own but that is represented in the class. The researchers should have an appointed *expert* who they can ask to clarify and check whatever they find out.

● The role of the researchers in every case is to find out not just how different people live, eat and dress but to establish the things that are important to people.

● Make opportunities for experts and researchers to talk at frequent intervals. The talks with classmates are likely to prove more informative than book or internet research, but the 'formal' research is also useful for providing a 'bigger picture' than one expert in the class can provide.

You Can... Make a difference in your community

Children should be at the heart of any community because they draw so many people and agencies together. Even young children can take some responsibility for playing their part as community members if we teach them how to do it. Before you begin a topic of this nature, ask parents and people in the community whether there are any particular issues relating to children, such as noise, litter, road safety, walking to school and rough play.

Thinking points

● Some of the group work here might be hard for Reception children to do without support, but let Year 1 children try to discuss and keep on task themselves. Use ideas from the *Speaking, Listening, Learning* pack to help give children skills for working in groups. A top priority is to give one child in each group the responsibility as 'chairperson'.

● Once children have come up with ideas, share them with parents and the wider school community. If you have a school council, ask that the ideas should be presented there.

Now try this

A starting point of books to share together:

● *Katie Morag* books by Mairi Hedderwick

● *Dogger* by Shirley Hughes

● *Lucy and Tom* or *Alfie* books by Shirley Hughes

● Jill Murphy's books about her family of bears (for example: *Peace at Last*) and elephants (for example: *An Evening Out*)

● *Ellen and Penguin and the New Baby* by Clara Vulliamy

● *Wilfrid Gordon McDonald Partridge* by Mem Fox

● *Once Upon an Ordinary School Day* by Colin McNaughton and Satoshi Kitamura

Tips, ideas and activities

● Introduce and discuss the idea of 'community'. Explain to children that they live in (at least) three communities: family, school and neighbourhood. Additionally, they may have church communities or play in football teams, or be members of rainbows, beavers or other groups of that nature.

● Discuss what being a member of a community might involve. Talk about relationships, respect, rights and responsibilities. What do the children see as their contribution to their communities?

● Read 'familiar setting' books about families and how they work together. Select books that show how different members of the community work together to make the community better, or where one family member makes a caring decision that makes another family member happy.

● As you read the books make notes about how relationships, respect, rights and responsibilities are demonstrated.

● Challenge the children to think of ways in which they could make the school community, or the neighbourhood if any particular issues were raised, a better place. Revisit the notes you made from your reading before children work in groups to consider their community: what makes them happy (for example: someone sharing something or lettering them join in a game)? What do other people do that makes them cross or sad (for example: being cross or spiteful, lying, hurting someone, teasing)? Ask them to think of the physical space: is there anything that upsets them (for example: graffiti, vandalism)? Or anything that particularly pleases them (for example: a play area, flowers)?

● When the groups have had their discussions, reconvene as a class and share the ideas. Discuss what children might be able to do to make the school community a happier, safer place.

You Can... Make a difference in your community

Children aged seven to eleven are old enough to take some responsibility for their environment and their community. The ideas on this page focus primarily on considering the school community, although the ideas could easily be adapted to consider the neighbourhood or a class community. The aim is for children to recognise their role and that they can make a difference.

Thinking points

● If your children find some of the group interaction hard, look through the ideas in the *Speaking, Listening, Learning* box. The objectives have been included in the Renewed Literacy Framework, so many of the ideas in the original handbook and posters are very useful – especially for group interaction, which children often find most difficult.

● Depending on the issues that are raised, you may want to set up a formal debate to talk about an idea. You will need to encourage the children to make sure that their research is secure.

Links to geography

QCA:

Awareness of, and suggestions for, improvements in the local environment is part of the geography curriculum through the primary years. The ideas on this page can be easily linked with any of the following units:

● Year 3, unit 6: Investigating our local area

● Year 4, unit 8: Improving the environment and unit 19: How and where do we spend our time?

● Years 3/4, unit 21: How can we improve the area we can see from our window?

● Year 5, unit 12: Should the high street be closed to traffic? and unit 20: Local traffic – an environmental issue.

Tips, ideas and activities

● Ask children to respond to the word 'community'. Can they define 'community'? Name communities of which they are members? Talk about what makes a community? Identify community leaders and explain what the leader's role entails?

● Discuss the implications of being a member of a community. Ensure that the discussions involve the ideas of relationships, respect, rights and responsibilities but explore additional ideas of common values.

● Let children work in groups to consider aspects of the school community that they like and those they dislike. Within their groups, let children debate whether personal dislikes such as 'no football in winter' are valid within a school community where everybody's rights need to be considered. Let a spokesperson from each group feed back what the group feels are the strengths of the school community and what should be changed.

● Let children go onto the internet and visit the websites of other schools in order to research whether there are similar issues and how the other schools have resolved them (for example: some schools have added a clause saying 'unless you have a change of shoes' to the football in winter ban).

● Once solutions have been researched and discussed in class, let the children compose a letter to the school leadership team or the school council explaining what the problem is, what research has been done and what solution is proposed.

● At a neighbourhood community level, the same process can be followed but the end result could be writing a letter to the local newspaper or a councillor. Whatever the level of the community issues, the important lesson for children is that their opinion does count and that they have responsibilities to their communities.

AGES 4–7

You Can... Promote reading in homes where there is no tradition of reading

In many schools there are 'hard to reach' families. Family members may have left school without having acquired good literacy skills and stayed away from school because of their own negative experiences. In order to break the cycle of poor literacy skills in these families, it is crucial to help to promote literacy in their homes.

Thinking points

● If you decide to do home visits, follow your school or local authority guidelines for your own safety.

● The majority of parents who are 'hard to reach' are not hostile and want their child to do well in school; they just don't know how to help. If you can help these parents to support their children you could make a real difference to the children's life chances.

The Family Reading Campaign

In order to develop reading in the home, the FRC recommends:

● agencies to work in partnership with parents

● children and young people should be helped to fulfil their potential and then they will start to enjoy reading

● different family cultures should be valued and the support offered should be flexible to suit families' varying needs

More information can be found at: www.literacytrust.org.uk /family reading.

Tips, ideas and activities

● Be prepared to make home visits as the children start school. Parents will often be more relaxed in their homes and most will appreciate you taking the time to call. Give the parents simple leaflets on reading with their children as well as the school phone number and a regular time when they can talk to you if they need additional advice.

● Make up packs of tapes, picture books and games. The games should be simple reading games based on the words and events in the book. Games for going home should have as few pieces as possible – but make sure that the pieces are replaceable. Simple lotto games, memory games, snap, board games, hide and seek games or race track games can be made to accompany most picture books.

● Make CD-ROMs and audio cassettes of your own picture books for children and parents to share. Young children will prefer to hear your familiar voice than to hear the voice of an unknown actor. Ting a glass when it's time to turn the page and allow the children a second or two to do it. Listening to the story together with their parents will be a precious time for the child.

● When you send home a game and book pack, make sure that the child has read the book in school and, ideally, played the game so that parents are not dependent on reading instructions. Don't send worksheets: the idea is that parents and children should be together as they play the game. These games are as much about bonding over the idea of reading as they are about reading aloud.

You Can... # Promote a culture of reading aloud

Reading aloud is an important skill to develop beyond Key Stage 1. One of the most telling ways of identifying if a child has fully understood a text is to hear them read aloud: their use of punctuation to guide intonation and expression is generally indicative of engagement and understanding. Create opportunities for your children to read aloud to you, to each other and to other members of the school community.

Thinking points

● One benefit of paired reading with younger children is that it gives your Key Stage 2 children an audience for their own writing. Once you have established reading partnerships, give your children opportunities to write for their younger partner. This could be a poem, a story or a non-fiction report text about something that the younger child finds interesting.

● Teach your children how to hear younger children read. Ask the younger children's class teacher to explain what she does when the children make an error, the kinds of questions she asks and how she congratulates the children.

Now try this

Paired reading can take a number of forms: carer and child; older and younger child; better and less-good same-age readers (but this often has negative effects on the self-esteem of the less-good reader); adult volunteers and children. Paired reading is a much more active reading partnership than a child reading to an adult.
For more information, look at one or more of these websites:

● www.childliteracy.com

● www.dyslexiamatters.co.uk/pairedreading.html

● www.fifepeerlearning.org/downloads/k2.pdf

● www.bitc.org.uk/news_media/paired_reading.html

Tips, ideas and activities

● Ask the children to help you to compile a list of the reading activities they do during the day in school. Highlight those that involve reading aloud. Discuss with children why there are comparatively few opportunities to read aloud.

● Many children in Key Stage 2 say that they don't like reading aloud. If this is true of your class, ask them to justify their opinion but don't accept 'because it's boring'. Try to unpick what the problem is: is it that the texts are too difficult and children make too many mistakes? Is it because they fear being criticised? Is it because they feel self-conscious?

● Discuss which audiences children would feel comfortable reading to without worrying. They are likely to say that they wouldn't mind reading to younger children. If this is the case, can you arrange set times each week when either your whole class, or a few children at a time, read with younger children? You may need to establish rotas, but both younger and older children seem to enjoy these sessions. Let your lowest achieving children read to younger low achieving children so that both children have a boost in self-confidence by the experience.

● If your older children are reading to the younger ones, why not increase the value of the session and let the younger children read to the older ones at the same time? You may well be surprised to find that your struggling readers are the most proficient at giving advice on useful strategies for reading.

● Once you have paired reading sessions going in school, you may want to consider other opportunities for older children to read aloud in the community. There may be a local nursery school, day care centre or visually impaired adult who would appreciate the opportunity for children to read aloud to them.

You Can... **Read aloud together**

Play scripts are favourite texts for reading aloud throughout the primary school. Children enjoy the experience of sharing a text, while each having their own part to read, and are generally more supportive of each other when reading play scripts than when reading other texts. They are also often more willing to read and reread a play script than a book. Play scripts aren't typically written for Reception aged children but they can still enjoy the same experience of reading together using some of the ideas below.

Thinking points

● To begin with, make sure that the play scripts are easier than other texts the children are reading: there is so much that is new in a play script that children shouldn't be worrying about the words.

● As children become more confident reading plays, introduce conventions of reading with expression. For many children, play scripts are their earliest experience of reading with expression.

Now try this
Creating a play script:

● Start with a familiar nursery rhyme. 'Pussy-cat, pussy-cat, where have you been?' or '1, 2, 3, 4, 5, once I caught a fish alive' are easy because the rhymes are already a dialogue. Alternatively, start with an action-driven short story that is known to the children.

● Prepare some pictures related to the main sequences of the story and help the children to re-tell the story in a simple way.

● Note the language they use and write it into your basic dialogue for each scene.

● Let all children read all of the play before you start giving groups their parts.

Tips, ideas and activities

● For their first play script or read-together text, read a text that is familiar to children. Reading schemes sometimes re-use stories with significant amounts of dialogue as play scripts so that children can read the stories first and then move on to the plays.

● When you first introduce children to play scripts, take time to teach them the conventions so they understand that they shouldn't read the character's name before they begin to speak and they know when they are expected to take their turn.

● Highlight different characters' parts in different colours to help children to be ready for their turn to speak when it comes.

● Very early reading books can often be turned into texts that can be read as play scripts. Look at the pictures and text together: Is there dialogue? Is there interaction between two characters? If the answer to either or these questions is yes, you can often rewrite the text in a play script form and paperclip the play over the conventional reading book pages. Use a Big Book for the first time you adapt a story so that you can work together to understand the new format.

● Alternatively, you can create a play script from scratch using an interactive whiteboard and some clip art characters. One clear advantage of creating your own plays scripts is that you can adapt the difficulty to cater for the phonic knowledge of your class.

● When you first introduce play scripts, let your class work in groups to chorally read each line. This will prevent the less-confident children from giving up before they even begin.

You Can... Promote a performance culture

Performing plays or poems is a powerful means of communication and most children will enjoy contributing. Teaching children about performance will require time and commitment, but it's a worthwhile investment.

Thinking points

● Performing can unlock the potential of many children. Drama techniques can be used to help even the shyest children to hide behind a character, become that character and leave their shy persona behind.

● If you are going to teach your children to perform, and give them time to rehearse, it will have implications for curriculum time unless you run an out-of-school-hours club. Balancing teaching performance, giving time for rehearsal and the rest of the curriculum can be tricky but it is worthwhile and the dividends can be extraordinary.

● Don't let children put on performances of materials they have written until they are skilled at performance. Unless both the material being performed and the performance are of a high quality, audiences will quickly lose interest.

Now try this
Performance opportunities

● Once your children are starting to enjoy performing, you may wish to let them enter some public competitions and examinations. Local authorities and libraries sometimes run poetry speaking competitions for schools and literary festivals will often have some community involvement too.

● Alternatively, you could contact LAMDA (www.lamda.org.uk) to find out more about their speech and drama exams and grades.

Tips, ideas and activities

● If your funds will allow it, invite a performance artist to come to school. If you can't afford to invite someone in, use websites to watch poetry performances online.

● Invite a professional performer to come and talk to your class. This could be a performance artist, someone from a local theatre company, a dance or drama teacher from the local secondary school. Ask your performer to talk to the children about performance issues including: voice projection, personal presentation, how to stand and move, how not to show your back to your audience, how to hold your hands, what to do if you want to giggle or cry and the importance of rehearsal.

● Plan a series of initial sessions for the children to perform to the class. Let them all plan to perform plays or poems – this is not a talent contest. Encourage them to perform in groups rather than one at a time.

● Give all children opportunities to perform in front of groups before they perform for the whole class. Give groups the responsibility of giving constructive feedback – you may need to coach them about how to do this.

● Give the children time to rehearse and improve their performance before they perform to the whole class.

● Once children have become experienced at performing in front of each other, give them opportunities to perform their poems, stories and plays to a wider audience. This could include a bigger group in school, a performance to parents or invitations to members of the community to come into school and watch them.

You Can... **Hold storytelling sessions**

In an age of intense visual stimulation, young children often find it hard to focus entirely on language, but storytelling sessions can give them the motivation and the opportunity to learn the necessary skills. Most children like stories and will be willing to sit and listen but make sure sessions are short and are not preceded or followed by a requirement to sit still.

Thinking points

● Research suggests that most children can concentrate for their age plus two in minutes. So, a seven-year-old can concentrate for no more than about nine minutes. Keep your storytelling sessions to within these boundaries before giving the children a short 'brain break' after which you can tell another story.

● Ask questions of different children after storytelling sessions in order to find out how much they took in of the story. Keep regular checks on children's ability to attend to the story and to make meaning: does it improve over the year?

Framework links

Storytelling is implicit in many of the objectives in strand 8 (Engaging with and Responding to Texts) of the Renewed Literacy Framework. This strand asks that children should:

● Listen with enjoyment to stories, sustain attentive listening and respond with relevant comments, questions or actions. (Reception)

● Visualise and comment on events, characters and ideas, making imaginative links to their own experience. (Year 1)

● Explain their reactions to texts, commenting on important aspects. (Year 2)

Tips, ideas and activities

● Organise regular storytelling sessions. Invite parents, members of your school community and members of the wider community to come and tell stories to groups of children. (Although remember that the children will always need to have a CRB checked adult with them.)

● Help children to know what to expect and how to behave when they have a storyteller with them. Agree on class rules such as 'don't interrupt to ask questions until the end'; 'you can't go to the toilet while the storyteller is speaking'; 'each child sits where you ask them to and doesn't move from that spot during the storytelling'.

● Younger children make more meaning from a book by looking at the pictures than by listening to the words; introduce storytelling slowly so that children have time to develop the skills they need to listen to a whole story.

● You may wish to invite all potential contributors to a workshop to talk to them about the skill of holding the attention of small children. Just because it's what you do every day doesn't make it easy for everyone! Some of your recruits may wish to use props like puppets as they tell their story. Encourage this, but discourage reading – that's a different session in the week.

● Remind your storytellers that younger children often have poorer memories than older ones, so too much embellishment of a story line will result in the children becoming lost since they won't be able to hold too many threads in their heads at one time. Remind them too that subtleties and sarcasm are wasted on younger children, so events in the story need to be clearly signposted.

You Can... Develop storytelling

Storytelling is an art form. Unlike reading a story, telling a story is different every time you do it. The skills involved in storytelling are also very different from those needed for reading, so children who are not good readers can prove to be gifted storytellers. Some of your hardest to reach families may be prepared to become involved in storytelling sessions and they may be able to share stories from different cultures with the children.

Thinking points

Give children access to anthologies of folk tales, or even retellings of Aesop's fables, as the basis for their early stories. These simply structured stories should give children the chance to focus on language and performing skills without having to worry too much about the order of events.

Now try this

Contact a story teller:
The most reliable method of finding a storyteller is by word-of-mouth from other schools. There isn't a national directory of storytellers as many are self-employed individuals who work in a small area. However, one of the organisations listed below may help:

● www.thelcis.org.uk is the London Centre for International Storytelling and is also the home of the Crick Crack Club: www.crickcrackclub.com.

● www.scottishstorytellingcentre.co.uk is the Scottish storytelling centre and http://storytelling.research.glam.ac.uk takes you to the John Ewart Evans Centre for Storytelling in Glamorgan.

Alternatively, visit your local library or, if all else fails, use a search engine to find storytellers nearby.

Tips, ideas and activities

● If you possibly can, invite a storyteller into school. Once children have experienced the power of a good story told by a live storyteller, they will understand the power of the art.

● Many storytellers are former teachers, so if your storyteller is willing to run workshops for your children, accept the offer.

● Teach children key strategies of a good storyteller:
  ○ Start with a good story. Most stories told by storytellers are stories from the oral tradition, and from a vast variety of cultures. Stories that have survived in this form, sometimes for centuries, have features that make them good stories for oral retelling. The adventures of a cartoon character may not have the same enduring qualities.
  ○ Know the key points in a story. Many storytellers practise telling stories using cards to sequence the events.
  ○ Develop a precise and expressive vocabulary. Illustrations must be drawn in the air between the storyteller and the audience and the storyteller needs a palette of words.
  ○ Be prepared to act. Storytellers must be able to use their whole bodies in the narratives in order that they can grip their audience.

● Let children begin by working in groups. Between them, the children can choose a story, plot its key points and agree on who is going to tell which episodes and in which order. The children should also agree how they want their audience to react to their story – a comedian may not be appropriate in a group that wishes to tell a ghost story.

● While you are involved in a storytelling project, invite family members and carers into school to tell stories. Focus particularly on family members with a culture outside of the UK, or on traveller communities where the culture is still oral rather than written. Inviting these community members into school will give status to their children and to their children's culture.

AGES 4–7

You Can... **Enjoy National Schools Film Week**

In October and November 2008, 400,000 children throughout the UK participated in National Schools Film Week. If your children didn't participate, why not? Films are screened all over the country and the only cost to schools is the cost of the coach: the viewing is completely free.

Thinking points

Be realistic in your expectations of how much the children can take in. If you know that they have a concentration span of about 10–15 minutes, how much of a 100-minute film will they be able to focus on? Watch them as they watch the film and look out for their 'brain break' strategies.

Framework and ICT links

The Renewed Literacy Framework recognises that, in this digital age, children need to become ICT literate and gives ten different categories where ICT adds value to the teaching of literacy and in which children need to become literate.

For children aged 4–7, ICT adds strength to every strand of the Framework, and film is of particular relevance to:

● Strands 1–4 – speaking, listening, group interaction and drama.

● Strand 7 – understanding and interpreting texts.

● Strand 8 – engaging with and responding to texts.

Tips, ideas and activities

● Contact the organisers, National Schools Film Week (www.nsfw.org), well in advance because the viewings get booked up early.

● If your children have never been to the cinema, prepare them for the experience by reading books and using orientation guides such as the one available at www.filmeducation.org. You may want to plan to turn your role-play area into a cinema on your return.

● Make a careful choice about the film you see. Although many are advertised as 'primary' they are not necessarily appropriate for four- to seven-year-olds. If possible, see the film yourself before committing your class to it.

● After the cinema visit, plan work around the visit as well as around the film. If the cinema will allow you to, take a digital camera and take photographs of the cinema itself for work in the classroom. For example:
   ○ Sequencing work following the sequence of experience you have on arrival at the cinema: foyer, ticket collection, sweet counter, corridor for queuing and toilets, auditorium.
   ○ Make zigzag books explaining the sequence of events in the cinema.

● Your library is likely to stock storybooks related to the films. If you want to buy books, most are available from good booksellers or online. Compare the book to the film. Ideas on page 51 can help you with this.

● Try having a 'cinema afternoon': make a room with blinds and an interactive whiteboard into a cinema auditorium. Have lines of chairs for children to sit on and let them watch a film together. Discuss the differences between watching a film in this school 'cinema' and in a proper cinema.

You Can... **Enjoy National Schools Film Week**

National Schools Film Week (www.nsfw.org) happens every Autumn and this year it is linked to reading. Films are screened all over the country for free and the only cost to schools is the cost of the coach. Taking your class to a cinema is a very unifying experience that can be built upon back in school, both in terms of a shared event and in terms of work related to the film.

Thinking points
● How film-literate are you? If you need a crash course in understanding and using film terminology , go to www.filmeducation.org/resources.html and download their study guides.

● Watch your children as they watch the film. Check that they are alert and aware of what is happening on screen. Many children are challenged when trying to make sense of the amount of stimulation in a film. Help them by increasing their understanding of some techniques of film-making.

Framework and ICT links
The Renewed Literacy Framework recognises that, in this digital age, children need to become ICT literate and it gives ten different categories where ICT adds value to the teaching of literacy and in which children need to become literate.

For children aged 7–11, ICT adds strength to every strand of the Framework, and film is of particular relevance to:

● Strands 1–4 – speaking, listening, group interaction and drama

● Strand 7 – understanding and interpreting texts

● Strand 8 – engaging with and responding to texts.

Tips, ideas and activities
● As you work using film, aim for children to gain a greater understanding of the elements that combine to make film so powerful.

● The UK film industry and the British Film Institute tend to produce resource packs of pictures, lesson plans and worksheets to accompany each of the films on show. Take advantage of these free resources in planning your unit of work.

● Many of the films shown during National Schools Film Week will also be available on DVD. Use this to continue to build on the learning experiences at the cinema during the week after you have seen the film on the big screen. Use clips of the film during discussions and let children select clips that explore different aspects of film.

● Discussions about the film should always include summarising the plot. Ask the children to use storyboards, which are used in the film industry, to show the key events in the story. Check that children haven't been seduced into confusing sub-plots with the main plot of the film.

● Revisit a particularly dramatic part of the film. Draw children's attention to the use of:
  ○ Music: *can the on-screen characters hear the music? What is its function? How does the scene change if you take the music away?*
  ○ Lighting: *how is the dramatic scene lit? Is it broad daylight, or are there shadows?* Discuss why the director might have chosen this lighting.
  ○ Camera angles: draw children's attention to the fact that some of the film shows scenes from far away so you can see a lot of setting around the action, whereas other parts of the film are shot from close up. *Which is used most in dramatic parts of the film?* Discuss why.

You Can... **Compare books and films**

Most major film releases are now accompanied by merchandising, including books in a variety of forms. In order to help children to develop film literacy, it is useful to spend time watching the film, then use whichever book is most appropriate to your class to discuss how books and films are the same and different.

Thinking points

Which film will you choose to watch with the children? A newly released blockbuster cartoon might not be the best choice as it is likely that some of the children
will have watched the film so many times that they will be able to speak the dialogue as they watch it and this will detract from the work you are doing together. 'Classic' films with a straightforward plot (for example: *The Lion King*, *Finding Nemo*, *Toy Story*, *Monsters Inc*) may be better bets since the books are still easily available and although children may have watched the film, they may not be able to recite it.

Recommended websites

● www.filmeducation.org has a number of archived 'study guides': these include guides for films that have previously been screened during National Schools Film Week.

● Sites such as www.disney.co.uk, www.thefilmfactory.co.uk, www.warnerbros.co.uk, www.dreamworksanimation.com, www.pixar.com and www.paramountpictures.co.uk have trailers of current and past films. You can watch the trailers from the UK and the US.

Use these sites too when choosing your film, as the sites generally include a useful synopsis of the film (about 100 words) which you can use as a guide when you're building your storyboard.

Tips, ideas and activities

● Have a 'cinema afternoon': make a room with blinds and an interactive whiteboard into a cinema auditorium. Have lines of chairs for children to sit on and let them watch a film together. It is important that the class watches the film at the same time because then they have a shared experience of the film which can be drawn on in your discussions.

● After the film, discuss the major events and draw your own 'class storyboard' of the film. This activity is likely to need a lot of teacher support and mediation since many children will have better memories of sub-plots (particularly if they are funny) than of the plot. However, working together through this activity will ensure that all of the children gain some understanding of the outline story of the film.

● Read the book of the film to the children. Check that all of the points you pulled out as critical to the plot are included in the book. If they aren't, discuss why they might have been omitted. The most likely reason is brevity: if you are reading a 24-page book of a 100-minute film, the book's author will need to have missed out some bits.

● Discuss what is the same between the book and the film, and talk about what is different. Key differences to discuss include the multi-sensory nature of the film, the number of different character voices, the lack of inward dialogue and thought in the film and the role of music.

● If you can, revisit parts of the film while you talk to illustrate the different points you are discussing.

● Invite children to write their own stories about the film of the book, based on the idea of storyboarding the events first: children can draw a sequence of pictures that tell the tale and then write the story.

● Put some of the children's books in your book corner alongside the book you shared together earlier.

You Can... Compare books and films

Part of the merchandising that now accompanies the release of every major film, is an array of books. Children in your class are likely to have some of these books. Invite the children to bring in and share the books so that everyone can see and enjoy them.

Thinking points
- Have any of the children ever read a book (for example: *Harry Potter*, *Lord of the Rings*, *The Golden Compass/ Northern Lights*), then seen the film and been disappointed? Discuss why this happens.

- Discuss with the children who are more entranced by film about the value of reading too. Also let those children have an opportunity to explain their preference and talk about why watching a film can be more a powerful experience.

Recommended websites
- Since film literacy is recognised as becoming so much more important, there are an increasing number of websites that will provide free resources to schools. For example, www.filmeducation.org has a number of archived 'study guides'. These include guides for films that have previously been screened during National Schools Film Week.

- www.pathe.co.uk has agreed to allow schools free access to its archive of films for educational use (access is only available from a school network).

- In addition, the big film distributors have trailers and advertising copy for recent and older films on their websites (www.disney.co.uk, www.thefilm factory.co.uk, www.warnerbros.co.uk, www.dreamworksanimation.com, www.pixar.com, www.fox.co.uk and www.paramountpictures.co.uk).

Tips, ideas and activities
- Read part of a book that is related to the film you have watched together and re-view that part of the film on DVD. Revisit where that part of the film comes in the story.

- Ask children to work in groups to think about what the film and the book have in common. Answers are likely to include: they both tell a story, the story has a similar narrative and chronology, and the characters and setting are the same.

- Now ask children to consider differences between the book and film. Apart from the obvious (the film has sound and movement) differences are often more subtle to tease out. Help the children to consider, for example:
  - The soundtrack. *How do the music and the sound effects contribute to enjoyment of the film? What does an author do in a book to create similar effects?*
  - The director edits the film to control the pace: action can be long and drawn out with wide-angled camera shots, or it can be rapid and choppy with close-ups on faces and action. Again, *how does an author create those effects in words?*
  - On film, characters' faces and bodies, as well as their language show us their emotions. *What do authors do to give the reader the same information?*
  - Authors are able to explain the inner-thought process of characters, which will often give motives for the actions. *How can film directors achieve this insight into a character's mind and soul?*
  - *Do you find images are more powerful in film, on the radio or in books?* Many children will assume that film is more powerful. Quote to them the child who reputedly said, 'I like stories on the radio best. The pictures are better.'

- The children will only be able to use a limited number of texts to explore these questions while you are completing this work, but encourage them to bear these questions in mind as they read and also as they write their own stories.

You Can... Learn about reading and writing from films

Once children have watched a film, even a short animated or cartoon story, extend the work into reading and writing.

Thinking points

Children write what they read. For all young writers there is a process of *imitate, innovate, invent*. Until they have imitated what they know, and then innovated to alter details, they are unlikely to invent. This may have implications for children's reading: if you only give them one reading scheme to read from, they will always write in the style of that reading scheme.

Framework links

The work on this page supports the focus of Strands 7–12 ('read and write for a range of purposes on paper and on screen.'), in particular:

● Foundation – children should listen to stories with enjoyment, sustain attentive listening, show an understanding of the elements of stories including character and sequence of events. Short films will achieve these objectives.

● Years 1 and 2 – short films and animations are useful when studying stories with familiar settings and traditional tales from other cultures. Look for some of the old *Words and Pictures* or *Jackanory* stories (www.bbcactive.com) and more modern character stories such as *Bob the Builder*, *Fireman Sam* and *Percy the Park Keeper*.

Tips, ideas and activities

● Watch short DVDs, or a longer film in episodes, on an interactive whiteboard and talk about what you can see on the screen. Derive as much information as you can about the characters.

● Ask children to think about *how they know* that Shrek is a good character whereas Lord Farquart isn't. What information are they given about what the characters look like, say and do that tells the viewer about the character? In addition, listen to the music that the character is linked to, look at the colours in their clothing and settings. Think about why it matters that the reader knows who are the good and the bad characters.

● Read a picture book together (it may be related to the screen characters or not) and think about *how you know* who are the good and the bad characters. What information are we given in a book that helps us to make these distinctions?

● For older children, repeat this process thinking about setting, and make use of both picture and non-picture books as well as guided reading books.

● Once children have experienced and discussed characters on screen and in books, ask them to role play different episodes from the film or book to explore the characters. In their role play, suggest that they consider how they move and speak as well as what they say and do.

● Ask children to draw and paint the different characters from the episodes you have been talking about. As they do so, ask them to think about which colours they want to use to represent the clothing and backgrounds of the good and the bad characters.

● Now ask children to write a description of each of the characters. For younger children, read their mark making and scribe powerful words and phrases for everyone to read.

● Finally ask children to write their own version of the episode you have been exploring. Ask the children to think about the characters, what they do, what they say and what they look like.

You Can... Learn about reading and writing from films

Studying film enhances the children's awareness of the writers' craft. They will realise that film directors only know how characters are feeling, what the setting should be and how dramatic a particular moment in the story is, because someone wrote it down first. Ask the question: what did the author do to give the film director the information?

Thinking points

● Many authors visualise stories before they begin to write. How do your children plan their stories? Having them all planning stories in the same way may restrict their authorial instincts.

● It is unlikely that reading journals can usefully record all information suggested here at once. Build the journals up over time so that they become a useful source of inspiration as the reader becomes a writer.

Framework links

The work on this page supports the focus of Strands 7–12 ('read and write for a range of purposes on paper and on screen.'), in particular:

● Year 3: myths and legends or adventure stories will lend themselves particularly well to work with film as many films, including *Shrek*, will support these genres.

● Year 4: films set in fantasy worlds are too numerous to mention. There are the sci-fi films such as *Star Wars* and *Spiderman* as well as the cartoons like *Shrek* and *The Incredibles*.

● Year 5: many stories by significant children's authors have been transposed to film, as have a number of myths and legends. Look for films such as *Lord of the Rings* or *Harry Potter*.

● Year 6: almost any film can be useful for studying fiction genres and extended narratives.

Tips, ideas and activities

● Use reference to films you have watched together to make a filmic distinction between story, plot and narrative.
  ○ The story is what the characters would say happened to them if they were asked. So, in *Finding Nemo* the story is about a little fish who is caught and put in a tank and his Dad who comes to rescue him.
  ○ The plot is the big theme, so the plot of *Finding Nemo* is the triumph of endurance, trust and co-operation.
  ○ The narrative is the combination of the story and the plot.

● Can children distinguish between story, plot and narrative in stories and books you read together? Can they distinguish between the narrator and the author?

● Ask children to keep reading journals of their independent reading books. In the journals, ask them to make notes about how authors show characters' reactions to events and ask them to look at dialogue, at actions and at reactions as well as at descriptions of the characters' reactions.

● Ask the children too to be aware of pace. *How does an author change and control the pace of events in a story?* In film, it's done with atmospheric music, with camera angle and with action. *How is it achieved in a story?* Point the children's attention at sentence constructions.

● In their journals, children should also make notes of information given about characters and settings. Many authors, particularly of children's books, choose not to write long and detailed description because readers often skim over them and pronounce them 'boring'. Ask children to focus on how they are given information about characters and settings without descriptions. Direct the children to look at the vocabulary and at the seemingly insignificant details we are told.

You Can... **Write better sentences**

As soon as children start to combine words to write, whether or not their writing can be read by another, encourage them to write in sentences. It is important that we explicitly work to teach children to extend their sentence structures.

Thinking points

● How good is the sentence structure and vocabulary of children in your class? Set high expectations for everyone to use more sophisticated language and don't enter into communications unless children are using language as well as they can.

● Make children ask explicitly for things they want from you. In a busy classroom, it's very easy to assume what children want and to give it to them. Their communication won't improve if they don't have to make an effort.

● Model using language that is slightly ahead of the language you want the children to use.

Framework links

Strand 11 is concerned with sentence structure and punctuation. Activities and investigations on this page will support children as they work towards these objectives.

● Foundation: begin to form simple sentences in writing, sometimes using punctuation.

● Year 1: compose and write simple sentences independently to communicate meaning and to use sentence punctuation.

● Year 2: write simple and compound sentences (joined by *and*, *but*, *or*, *so*) as well as subordination in relation to time and reason (sentences joined by *because* or time phrases like *then*, *next*).

Tips, ideas and activities

Use investigations to begin to help children to understand how sentences are built. For example:

● Using words and pictures, create a simple sentence like: *The cat sat on the mat.*

● Ask children to suggest other words we could use instead of *cat*. Give them options of other animals, but also words like *jump*, *saw*, *it*. *Why won't these words take the place of 'cat'?*

● Repeat for other words in the sentence: *which words can be used to replace 'sat'? 'on'?'the'? 'mat'?* This activity develops an awareness of word classes.

● Teach children to use connectives or joining words. Start a sentence *The cat sat on the mat because…* and record children's suggested sentence endings. Change the connective: *The cat sat on the mat until… so… but… then…* As you play these games, discuss what's not possible as well as what is possible. Give the children a chance to explore rather than simply giving them instructions.

● Teach adjectives by asking children to describe all manner of things in the classroom. As well as using adjectives after the noun (for example, *The monster is green*) encourage use before the noun (for example, *The green monster stomped down the hill*). A good collection of adjectives is crucial for a writer.

● Introduce powerful verbs during PE or drama lessons. Can the children *go, walk, run, stagger, stamp, tiptoe, skip*? Can they *say, shout, ask, whisper, groan*?

● Once you have introduced a range of adjectives, verbs and connectives, keep pointing them out in reading. If you hear children uttering sentences including these words, write the sentences out and display them to show that you value the use of more interesting language and sentences.

You Can... **Write better sentences**

The key differences between non-fiction text types are buried in the sentence constructions used. The most fundamental difference between instructions and recount is the tense and person (instructions are second person, present tense; recounts are generally first person, past tense); explanations differ from reports in the types of connectives used. Teach children to take control of the sentences they use.

Thinking points

● How good is the spoken language of children in your class? This is not a question about elocution but of sentence structure and vocabulary. Set high expectations for more sophisticated language.

● When you read with children, increase their sensitivity to well-constructed sentences. Explain explicitly what it is about the sentence that 'works'.

● Enjoy sessions where you all 'speak like a book', using a more refined vocabulary and a wider range of more formal sentence structures.

● Make a point of valuing interesting sentences in children's writing. .

Framework links

Strand 11 is concerned with sentence structure and punctuation. Activities and investigations on this page will support children as they work towards these objectives.

● Year 3: compose sentences using adjectives, verbs and nouns for precision, clarity and impact.

● Year 4: clarify meaning by using varied sentence structures (phrases, clauses and adverbials).

● Year 5: adapt sentence construction to different text-types, purposes and readers.

● Year 6: express subtle differences of meaning by constructing sentences in varied ways.

Tips, ideas and activities

Use investigations to help children to understand how sentences are built. For example:

● If children can write simple sentences, compound sentences and complex sentences joined by *because* and some adverbials of time they can get a level 2B at the end of Year 2. In order to move through level 3 and level 4, children need to be able to demonstrate not just that they *can* write a greater variety of sentences but that they can make controlled choices about the sentence structures they use. That element of *control* is critical.

● Children need to be given opportunities to investigate different sentence types and how to change and improve them. Investigations can include games that involve playing with sentences, for example:
  ○ Children start by writing a simple sentence on their whiteboard.
  ○ Add an adjective. (Talk about where in the sentence in might go.)
  ○ Add an adverb. (*Where might that go?*)
  ○ Rub out the adverb and put it somewhere else. (*Where else can it go?*)
  ○ Add a *because* clause.
  ○ Move the *because* clause to the beginning of the sentence.
  ○ Add another subordinate clause to the end of the sentence....

● Write a set of unconnected words, such as: fire, rolled, astronaut, trapeze, golden. Ask children to write a meaningful sentence including the words.

● Give children a topic such as 'space' and ask them to write the opening sentence of a report, a recount, a persuasive text, a discussion, a horror story, an adventure story.

● There are endless variations on games like these, all of which teach children to enjoy language and help them to understand their own power in controlling and shaping sentences.

You Can... **Write better stories**

December is a time for magical stories based on celebrations. Whatever the children's religions or cultures, there are many good stories for this time of year often published from many different perspectives. This is the ideal opportunity for teaching your children that the same story can be told in many different ways and that each retelling shows you something new and fresh about a familiar story.

Thinking points

● If you have children in your class whose first language isn't English, ask them if they or their carers have a copy of a celebration story in their first language. Can they or their carers come and share the story in that language? Look for dual-language versions.

● Look on the internet and in good bookshops for colourfully illustrated stories about Diwali, Hanukkah, Ramadan, Chinese New Year.

Now try this
Assessing talk for writing:

As you listen to the children talk through role play and sequencing activities, sample their talk and assess it against learning objectives for the children. For example:

● Are they talking in sentences or sentence-like structures?

● Are they able to use a variety of connectives and sentence structures?

● Are they mimicking language from the books? Can they vary the language?

● Can they use adjectives and precise nouns and verbs to make their language more interesting?

● Are they able to use language for negotiation within the group?

● Can they use intonation, expression and body language to make their oral story telling more interesting?

Tips, ideas and activities

● Read different versions of celebration stories to your children. Each time you read to them, talk about what was familiar and what was new.

● Once the children have had the opportunity to hear a story many times, give them the opportunity to role play aspects of it. Approach this in a number of different ways. You can:
  ● Tell the story while the children mime the events.
  ● Give children scripts, based on versions of the story you have read together, to read.
  ● Ask a narrator to take charge of each group of actors.
  ● Let the children organise their own retelling of the story.
  ● Give the children puppets or drawings to use to tell the story.

● Allow the children time to explore the story in different ways until good storytelling language becomes part of their role play.

● Create pictures for sequencing to retell part of the story. Choose an appropriate number of pictures for the age and stage of your children. Let children work in pairs to sequence the pictures and to tell the story to each other.

● Depending on the writing level of your children, you can now ask them to write the story. You can do this by:
  ● Using a story-building program, such as *Clicker*, to give them sentence frames to retell the story. Use the sentence structures from the children's language as if they were retelling the story.
  ● Giving them the pictures that they sequenced and asking them to retell the story in a zigzag book.
  ● Giving them one picture to act as a prompt, together with a list of useful words, and asking them to write the story.

● Although you probably can't afford the time to do this amount of preparation every time the children write, the quality of writing this kind of preparation should produce can act as a benchmark for future writing.

You Can... **Write better stories**

Many children complain 'I don't know what to write.' What can we, as teachers, do to ensure that children do know what to write? And how can we make sure that the stories they write for us are as good as they can be? The answer is to ask them to start writing later in the writing process.

Thinking points

● The majority of children can't sustain quality writing for more than about 30–50 minutes at a time. How much can they realistically write in that time? Ask them to find out not only how many words, but what that number of words looks like.

● How many 'parts' do you expect in a story? Beginning, middle, end? Beginning, problem, climax, resolution, ending? Let your children experiment to see how many lines of writing each part might be. It's useful for children to have an idea of how much they are expecting to write so they don't get distracted, write too much in the introduction and never finish the story.

Now try this

Using response partners:

Response partners are useful in the writing process, partly because they can take the pressure off you to listen and respond to 30 stories. More importantly, response partners train children to take on the responsibility of assessor and editor. The skills they learn working on their friends' stories will benefit their own writing.

Response partners guidelines:

● Not to spot more than five errors.

● To make two useful, positive comments ('I like your idea and I think it's good' is NOT useful).

● To suggest one key thing that will improve the story.

Tips, ideas and activities

● There is significant evidence to show that many children, particularly boys, don't multi-task well when they are writing. They become overwhelmed by the number of things they have to worry about: plot, written style, sentence construction, vocabulary choice, spelling, punctuation, handwriting, targets and learning objectives, so they give up. The way to improve matters is to reduce the pressure at each stage in the writing process.

● Before children put pencil to paper they should have read texts similar to the one they are going to write and completed some analysis of them. Children also need to know some of the features and expectations of the genre: what are the expectations of language structure and vocabulary? Of theme and plot? Of characters and settings? How should their reader feel at the end of the story? Who is their reader most likely to be?

● Once children have this basic toolkit of knowledge about the genre, they are ready to begin to respond to your stimulus. How do you think they will respond most creatively? Through drama, role play, art, dance, music? Then let children talk through their ideas with response partners. Train response partners to give constructive responses.

● Now let children plan. How many different planning styles have your children learned? Can they draw storyboards or story mountains? Have they learned to mind map their plans? Once children have practised using a range of planning tools, let them choose which will be most useful to them for each story. Emphasise planning time should not be more than about 5–10 minutes.

● Finally, before the children begin to write, ask them to tell their story to their response partner. The important thing at this stage is to practise the rhythms of the language for writing and to finalise the ideas, trying to get as much balance as possible without giving too much detail at any point.

● Now when the children begin to write, they do know what to write and how to write it. The number of things to worry about has been reduced.

You Can... **Become a better writer**

Teaching writing is one of the most rewarding parts of teaching. Giving children the power to write and to communicate their ideas is giving them a life-changing skill. Teach children to use a keyboard efficiently and if spelling continues to be a problem, let children word-process their writing. Above all, be positive and enthusiastic about teaching writing. Give children authentic writing tasks and let them explore their ideas and creativity through writing.

Thinking points

● What scaffolding is in place when you ask children to write? Have you taught them about the kind of writing they are going to do? Do they know the purpose for their writing? And its audience? Even the youngest writer should know the answer to these questions before they begin to write.

● Making writing frames for reception children is useful and easy: divide a piece of paper into 4 columns and tell children to put a time in the first column (today), a person in the second column (I), what they did in the third column (went for a walk) and a place in the fourth column (in the park). Children can write multiple sentences in this frame to create a recount or a story.

Recommended websites

Writing is such a high profile activity now and, because there is a clear expectation that some of the writing is completed using ICT, a number of websites are available to give you support, or to give children models and ideas for writing. These sites may help:

● www.topmarks.co.uk/Interactive.aspx?s=literacy

● www.ngfl-cymru.org.uk

● www.tre.ngfl.gov.uk

● www.kented.org.uk/ngfl/ict/bett

● www.bgfl.org

● www.learninggrids.com/uk

Tips, ideas and activities

Use the theme of festivals to develop different kinds of writing:

● Make lists: in December children's television channels seem to be dawn-to-dusk advertisements and children are assailed by things they should *want* or *need*. Let children write lists of the three things they want to give mummy; of four things for their brother, and so on. Children can use catalogues for inspiration and pictures, but make sure that the end result is in the form of a list.

● Write letters: thank you letters are becoming unfashionable, but teach your children how to write thank you letters and see if we can restart this practice. Children can write to say thank you for... a good breakfast, a warm pair of gloves, a morning kiss, a friend at playtime. There are many reasons to be grateful, so teach your children how to express this in a letter.

● Write reports: *what do children know about reasons for celebrating? Why is it darker at this time of year? Why do we need to wear coats in winter? Why do we need to feed the birds?* Once you have taught children to ask questions and given them strategies for finding answers – even if the strategies are asking adults for information – expect to have the answers written for you. Make a class book of your questions and answers for everyone to read and enjoy.

● Write recounts: What did the children do yesterday? This morning? At the weekend? Check that they understand the language and give them simple sentence frames if necessary.

● Write stories: The most important message about asking young children to write stories is that they shouldn't be asked to write until they have had the chance to act, draw, dance and, above all, to speak their story. When children write, they should already know what they plan to say otherwise the thought processes necessary to form the letters and sound out the words will interfere with those needed to create a story.

You Can... **Become a better writer**

Make writing exciting in your class and give it a high status. If you are excited and enthusiastic about writing, your children will be too and the standards of writing will improve. There are so many ideas now to support children who struggle to write, that you can realistically believe that all children in your class are writers and that your job is to help them to live up to their potential.

Thinking points

● Recognise the distinction between children who struggle to write and those who are lazy and need to make more effort. Talk to the children to find out where the problems lie: is it with the ideas? with the spelling? with sentence construction? Solutions are available for each of the problems, but first the blocks to progress have to be identified and acknowledged.

● What do you want from your children as writers? You need to have clear targets in mind and only then can you start planning for your targets to be achieved.

Now try this

Children for whom writing is a particular challenge may benefit from using some form of ICT. Unless the child has a particular problem holding a pen, it is useful to expect some level of handwriting. Redrafting texts is usually a good place to make sure that children write by hand. ICT options can include:

● Allow children to record their texts or use digital cameras/ video recorders to create sequences before beginning to write their text.

● Using speech recognition software. *Dragon Naturally Speaking* (www.nuance.co.uk) is a popular option but *Sphinx 4* (http:// cmusphinx.sourceforge.net/sphinx4) is free.

● Allow dyslexic children access to a laptop, which will underline their spelling errors so that they can correct them when they are ready.

Tips, ideas and activities

● Have a free and frank exchange of opinions with your class: what is it about writing that they like/ dislike?, that they find easy/ challenging? Use the information from this conversation to plan writing activities. Make them as interesting and as motivational as you can. If possible, make writing fun!

● Let children set their own targets for improving their writing. Before you do this it is useful to share the kinds of targets that you would think are useful, but give the children the opportunity to set their own targets before you impose yours. Setting and working towards your own targets is very motivational for most children.

● Make sure that children always know the purpose and audience for every piece of writing they do. Even if the audience is you, let the children know that, but tell them what you want their piece of writing to do to transform your life. Do you wish to be informed… entertained… scared… convinced…? Discuss the implications of that purpose on their writing. Check that they are familiar with the key points and conventions of the text type of genre.

● Most importantly, never let children dive into a piece of writing without a plan and without having spoken the writing aloud first. The plan doesn't need to be on paper and it certainly doesn't need to be in neat boxes, but the children should know where the writing is going and what it will say before they begin. Speaking the writing can be done in a myriad of ways: through drama, role play, art; with a response partner or trusted adult; simply mumbled through at the table to themselves. But until a child has spoken and heard the rhythm of the writing, the choice of words and sentences, they are unlikely to be able to do their best.

Every Child Matters and reading

The *Every Child Matters* (*ECM*) agenda should be at the heart of all teaching and learning including reading. The renewed Primary Framework for literacy has embedded the principles of *ECM* into their guidelines so that everyone involved in teaching children aged from 3 to 11 can put the principles into practice and continue to raise standards. This book has been written to take the *ECM* outcomes into account. It achieves this in the following ways:

Staying Safe
We teach our children to stay safe in a number of ways, not the least of which is by teaching them to ask questions and to think independently. Throughout the book, and from Foundation Stage to Key Stage 2, there are suggested activities that encourage children to ask questions in order that they have some responsibility and control over what they learn.

Being Healthy
The theme of being healthy, both in mind and body, is developed through a number of units in this book. in particular 'Chapter 2: You can... read to develop mind and body' and 'Chapter 5: You can... Read the game', where children are encouraged to participate in sport and other activities during the summer holidays.

Enjoying and Achieving
This outcome is the main focus of this book and of every unit in it: in order for children to enjoy and achieve in school and society today they need to be able to read and write. One of our aims therefore should be to promote reading as being at the heart of enjoying and achieving.

Economic Well-being
For children in primary schools, this is generally seen as being linked to enjoying and achieving: children who do well at school have a better chance of attaining economic well-being. Activities in this book that focus on strengthening bonds between parents and children, particularly in homes where reading is not a traditional activity, potentially contribute to the economic well-being of the entire family.

Making a Positive Contribution
Community and cultural links are well represented in this book. Suggested activities, which make children aware of events in school and in the wider community, which promote discussion, negotiation and action and which help children to take some responsibility for events outside of their immediate lives, all teach them how to make a positive contribution within their different communities.

Assessment for Learning

Assessment for Learning (AfL) is an approach to assessment that promotes future learning, rather than focusing on how much children have learned in the past. The Excellence and Enjoyment Strategy (DfES 2003) first spread the AfL message, and AfL is increasingly being recognised as the most powerful classroom tool for teaching and learning.

At the heart of AfL are four attributes:
- Children are aware of targets and learning outcomes for every lesson.
- Children know what they have to do to improve their own learning.
- Marking and feedback promote future learning as opposed to simply commenting on what has already been achieved.
- Children are engaged in peer- and self-assessment.

These four attributes are threaded throughout these units, which assumes AfL as the most informative assessment regime for the activities.

One feature of a classroom in which AfL is being successfully practised is that learning and knowledge are 'owned' by the learners. In many classrooms, even those in which the AfL attributes seem to be evident, teachers still control the learning and disseminate it to the children in carefully controlled amounts. This is a very familiar and safe way of teaching and it's also efficient since you can ensure that learners learn what you, the teacher, deems to be important. The mark of a classroom in which the learners own at least some of the learning, is in the questions asked by the learners. These classrooms are 'learning communities' in which adults and children learn alongside each other. Classroom philosophies like Mantle of the Expert (www.mantleoftheexpert.com), Philosophy for Children (www.sapere.org.uk/) and Building Learning Power (www.buildinglearningpower.co.uk) are all aimed at trying to develop classroom learning communities and giving learners responsibility for some of their learning by teaching them to ask the questions. While this book is too short – and with a different main focus – to introduce any particular classroom philosophy, there is a consistent aim of encouraging the children to ask questions and to initiate learning.

Giving children opportunities for independent research is another route for enabling them to take on some responsibility for their learning. For this, a good school library is important but access to ICT media and the internet may be even more so. However, if you are expecting your children to learn from ICT, you will need to give them the skills and strategies they need to use these media successfully. Strategies for gaining information from a printed page are different to those for gaining information from an electronic one.

Curriculum Links

Unit No	In F/KS1 You can	Relevant to curriculum areas	Unit No	In KS2 You can	Relevant to curriculum areas
1	Provide daily opportunities to read in F/KS1	ICT	2	Provide sustained opportunities to read in KS2	ICT; numeracy
3	Use environmental print	ICT; numeracy	4	Use newspapers	
5	Sell It!	ICT	6	Judge the advert	
7	Put nursery rhymes in the news	ICT	8	Rewrite nursery rhyme history	ICT
9	Support reading with parents	SEAL	10	Support reading at home	ICT; SEAL
11	Answer questions about being healthy	ICT; science; SEAL	12	Find out about being healthy	ICT; science; SEAL
13	Find out about games and sports	ICT; science; PE	14	Become a Reading Champion	PE
15	Create imaginary worlds	art; music	16	Explore imaginary worlds	art; music; ICT
17	Find out about other countries	ICT; geography; SEAL	18	Find out about other countries	ICT; geography; SEAL
19	Have a summer reading challenge	SEAL	20	Have a summer reading challenge	ICT; SEAL
21	Enjoy songs and rhymes	ICT; history; science	22	Be positive about poetry	ICT
23	Teach reading skills through songs and rhymes	music	24	Develop reading skills through poetry and rhyme	SEAL
25	Develop confident readers through songs and rhyme	ICT	26	Develop self-esteem using poetry and rhyme	SEAL
27	Find out about holiday sports and activities	ICT; SEAL	28	Keep up to date with your team	ICT; PE
29	Organise an Olympics	ICT; PE	30	Find out about the Olympics	geography; numeracy
31	Turn children into readers	SEAL	32	Turn children into readers	
33	Explore different cultures	SEAL	34	Find out about different cultures	SEAL; ICT; RE
35	Make a difference in your community	SEAL	36	Make a difference in Your community	SEAL; geography
37	Promote reading in homes with no tradition of reading		38	Promote a culture of reading aloud	
39	Read aloud together		40	Promote a performance culture	
41	Hold storytelling sessions		42	Develop storytelling	
43	Enjoy National Schools Film Week	ICT	44	Enjoy National Schools Film Week	ICT
45	Compare books and film	ICT	46	Compare books and film	ICT
47	Learn about reading and writing from film	ICT	48	Learn about reading and writing from film	ICT
49	Write better sentences		50	Write better sentences	
51	Become a better writer	ICT; SEAL; RE	52	Become a better writer	ICT
53	Write better stories	RE; SEAL	54	Write better stories	

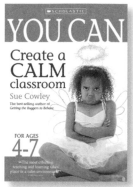